Lorraine Hansberry

Lorraine Hansberry
Courtesy Estate of Robert Nemiroff

LORRAINE HANSBERRY

A Research and Production Sourcebook

Richard M. Leeson

Modern Dramatists Research and Production
Sourcebooks, Number 13
William W. Demastes, Series Adviser

GREENWOOD PRESS
Westport, Connecticut • London

Library of Congress Cataloging-in-Publication Data

Leeson, Richard M., 1949–
    Lorraine Hansberry : a research and production sourcebook /
Richard M. Leeson.
        p.   cm.—(Modern dramatists research and production
sourcebooks, ISSN 1055–999X ; no. 13)
    Includes bibliographical references and indexes.
    ISBN 0–313–29312–0 (alk. paper)
    1. Hansberry, Lorraine, 1930–1965—Bibliography.   2. Women and
literature—United States—Bibliography.   3. Afro-Americans in
literature—Bibliography.   I. Title.   II. Series.
Z8385.64.L44   1997
[PS3515.A515]
016.812′54—dc21   97–12283

British Library Cataloguing in Publication data is available.

Library of Congress Catalog Card Number: 97–12283
ISBN: 0–313–29312–0
ISSN: 1055–999X

First published in 1997

Greenwood Press, 88 Post Road West, Westport, CT 06881
An imprint of Greenwood Publishing Group, Inc.

Printed in the United States of America

The paper used in this book complies with the
Permanent Paper Standard issued by the National
Information Standards Organization (Z39.48–1984).

10 9 8 7 6 5 4 3 2

Contents

Preface

Lorraine Hansberry: A Research and Production Sourcebook has not only been written as a useful reference guide, but also as a means by which scholars and interested readers may gain a critical sense and understanding of the scope of Lorraine Hansberry's career and her accomplishments as a dramatist. Consequently, in addition to including an overview of her personal and professional life, thorough and detailed annotated bibliographies of theatrical reviews and other secondary sources, thoughtful summaries of the plays, and production/credit information, the book also contains an essay for each published play which carefully reviews its critical reception. Additionally, when appropriate, some attention has been given to screen and television adaptations of her works. Finally, in an effort to make the information contained herein as accessible as possible, entries in the bibliographies have been coded for quick cross-referencing, and both *author* and *general* indexes have been included.

Acknowledgments

Anyone doing a study such as this owes a great deal to scholars and critics who have written eloquently on the life and art of Lorraine Hansberry. In this regard, I am indebted to the scholarship of Steven R. Carter (*Hansberry's Drama: Commitment and Complexity*), Anne Cheney (*Lorraine Hansberry*) and Margaret B. Wilkerson, for her many insightful articles on Hansberry's work. For the efforts of these three, and of many others, I am grateful.

I also want to thank those at Fort Hays State University who helped me with this project: Dr. James Forsythe and the Graduate School, for a generous research grant; the staff of Forsyth Library, in particular Phyllis Schmidt, Carolyn Herrman, Lawrence "Mac" Reed, and Christine Gilson, for their cheerful, efficient assistance; and Clifford Edwards, chairman of the Department of English, for his encouragement and support. I am also grateful to Fort Hays State University and the Kansas Board of Regents for granting me a sabbatical to complete research for this book.

In addition, I want to extend special appreciation to LouAnn Gottschalk, my research assistant, and JoAnn Crist, my expert secretary, without whom the completion of this study would have been practically impossible.

Finally, I want to once again thank those who are the most important of all: Mom, Dad, and John; Al and Laura. As I did with *William Inge: A Research and Production Sourcebook*, I now dedicate *Lorraine Hansberry: A Research and Production Sourcebook* to them.

A Note on Codes
and Numbering

"A" -- A prefix identifying references to Lorraine Hansberry's fiction and poetry, listed alphabetically in Section II of the chapter "Primary Bibliography: Writings by Hansberry."

"B" -- A prefix identifying references to Lorraine Hansberry's non-fiction, listed alphabetically and selectively annotated in Section III of the chapter "Primary Bibliography: Writings by Hansberry."

"P" -- A prefix identifying references to Lorraine Hansberry's dramatic writings, listed alphabetically in Section I of the chapter "Primary Bibliography: Writings by Hansberry."

"R" -- A prefix identifying reviews, annotated and arranged play by play in the chapter "Secondary Bibliography: Reviews."

"S" -- A prefix identifying other secondary materials, annotated and chronologically arranged in the chapter "Secondary Bibliography: Books, Articles, Sections."

Chronology

1930   Lorraine Vivian Hansberry, born May 19 in Chicago, Illinois to Carl A. Hansberry and Nannie Perry Hansberry--their fourth and youngest child.

1935   Is hassled at school by poverty-stricken classmates who resent the new, white fur coat she wears.

1938   Carl Hansberry buys a home in a white neighborhood and family suffers hostility and violence from neighbors. Illinois court upholds restrictive real estate covenant based on race and evicts them. Carl Hansberry takes case to the Supreme Court.

1940   Carl Hansberry and NAACP lawyers win their case before the Supreme Court (Hansberry vs. Lee) on November 12.

1944   Graduates from elementary school; enters Englewood High School and excels in English, history, and debate.

1946   Carl Hansberry dies in Mexico while planning to move his family there to avoid U.S. racism.

1947   Is elected president of high school debating society.

1948   After graduating from high school, attends the University of Wisconsin and studies stage design, drama, art, and literature. Sees *Juno and the Paycock* and becomes chairperson of the Young Progressives.

1949   Studies painting at the University of Guadalajara extension campus in Ajijc, Mexico and at the Mexican Art Workshop during the summer.

1950   Studies art during the summer at Roosevelt University. Having decided not to return to the University of Wisconsin, moves to New York City and briefly takes courses in short story writing, jewelry making, and photography at the New School for Social Research. Begins work on Paul Robeson's *Freedom* and develops more intense interests in social issues and politics affecting minorities.

1951   Moves to Harlem and becomes active in various freedom causes, including a delegation seeking to stop the execution of William McGee, a convicted (alleged) rapist in Mississippi.

1952   Becomes associate editor of *Freedom* and presents a speech at the Intercontinental Peace Conference in Montevideo, Uruguay for Paul Robeson, whose passport had been revoked by the State Department. Her passport is consequently revoked, as well. Meets Robert Nemiroff, an aspiring writer, while he was picketing against racial discrimination at New York University, where he was a graduate student in history and English.

1953   Marries Robert Nemiroff on June 20. While continuing to write short pieces, resigns job at *Freedom* to devote more time to playwriting. Settles with husband in Greenwich Village and studies with W.E.B. DuBois at the Jefferson School for Social Science.

1953-1956   She and Nemiroff work various odd jobs, Hansberry continuing to write and he taking a job in promotions at Avon Books.

1956   Nemiroff's popular song "Cindy, Oh Cindy" becomes a
            hit. When he takes a job managing a music publishing
            firm owned by Philip Rose, Hansberry is free to write full
            time. She begins work on "The Crystal Stair," which de-
            velops into *A Raisin in the Sun*.

1957   Reads the completed *A Raisin in the Sun* to Philip Rose,
            who decides to produce it. Rose secures Lloyd Richards
            to direct the play which will star Sidney Poitier. One of
            several letters to homosexual publications concerning the
            suppression of women and homosexuals (all written in
            anonymity) appears in *The Ladder*, a lesbian journal.

1959   Unable to secure a Broadway theater, backers arrange for
            A Raisin in the Sun to try out in various cities, where it is
            well received. Opens on Broadway at the Ethel Barry-
            more on March 11. The first play by a black woman to
            be produced on Broadway, it wins the New York Critics
            Circle Award as the best drama of the year. Movie rights
            are sold to Columbia Pictures.

1960   Hansberry writes and submits screenplays of *A Raisin in
            the Sun* that more clearly emphasize racial themes than
            did the Broadway production. Columbia Pictures insists
            on a less controversial script more in line with the stage
            play. Is commissioned by NBC to write what becomes
            The Drinking Gourd, which is deemed too controversial
            and is never produced. Works on *Toussaint*, *The Sign in
            Jenny Reed's Window* (which becomes *The Sign in Sid-
            ney Brustein's Window*), and *Les Blancs*.

1961   Moves to Croton-on-Hudson in New York. Film version
            of *A Raisin in the Sun* is nominated by the Screen Actors
            Writers Guild for the best screenplay of the year and wins
            an award at the Cannes Film Festival.

1962   Helps to garner support for the Student Non-violent
            Coordinating Committee (SNCC). Condemns the Cuban
            Missile Crisis and the House Un-American Activities
            Committee. Completes *What Use Are Flowers?*

1963   Becomes ill with cancer and undergoes two operations.
          Along with other black leaders, artists, and intellectuals,
          has a widely publicized and disappointing meeting on ra-
          cial issues with Attorney General Robert Kennedy. Scene
          from *Les Blancs*, directed by Arthur Penn, is staged at
          the Actors Studio Writers Workshop.

1964   Marriage to Nemiroff ends in a congenial, secret divorce.
          They continue to collaborate as she writes and takes
          radiation and chemotherapy treatments. Delivers what
          became known as the "To Be Young, Gifted and Black"
          speech to the winners of a writing contest sponsored by
          the United Negro College Fund. Publishes *The
          Movement: Documentary of a Struggle for Equality*, a
          book of photos with commentary by Hansberry, the pro-
          ceeds of which go to SNCC. *The Sign in Sidney
          Brustein's Window*, co-produced by Robert Nemiroff,
          opens October 15 at the Longacre Theatre. After it re-
          ceives mixed reviews, actors and those sympathetic to the
          ailing playwright and her serious work, collaborate and
          sacrifice to keep the play running for a total of one-hun-
          dred and one performances.

1965   Dies of cancer on January 12 at the age of thirty-four.
          The Sign in Sidney Brustein's Window closes on this
          day.

1969   *To Be Young, Gifted and Black* opens at the Cherry Lane
          Theater in New York on January 2.

1970   *Les Blancs* opens at the Longacre Theatre in New York
          on November 15.

1973   Musical *Raisin* opens at the 46th Street Theatre on
          October 18.

Life and Career

In his poignant reminiscence of Lorraine Hansberry, who died at the age of 34 in 1965, James Baldwin (S22) remarked that this "small, dark girl, with her wit, her wonder, and her eloquent compassion" left this life too soon. "When so bright a light goes out so early," he noted, we are "left with a sorrow and a wonder that speculation cannot assuage." How quickly had she appeared and departed! Only a few years earlier, in 1959, her first-produced play, *A Raisin in the Sun*, was met with the enthusiastic praise of Broadway critics and audiences alike. It was the first, and longest running, play by an African-American woman to be produced on Broadway. And when it won the New York Drama Circle Award for the best new drama that year, Hansberry became the first black woman and the youngest recipient ever to receive that honor.

    A Raisin in the Sun was a powerful exploration of racial prejudice and discrimination that demonstrated the twenty-nine-year-old Hansberry's commitment to social justice which had been forged in her years earlier while growing up on the Southside of Chicago.

    Born on May 19, 1930, Lorraine Vivian Hansberry was the youngest of four children of Carl Augustus and Nanny Perry Hansberry. Carl Hansberry, the son of teachers, had come north from Mississippi seeking prosperity, and he found it. Early on, he became an accountant for the first black bank in Chicago and then founded one of his own. Continuing to prosper, he invested wisely in ghetto real estate and rental property (S87), growing wealthy, in part, by converting larger apartments to smaller ones, each containing a "kitchenette." By renting these small apartments (not unlike the one occupied by the Youngers in *A Raisin in the Sun*) to his fellow blacks, he was able to provide a comfortable income for his family (S140).

Hansberry's mother, who met her husband while working in his bank, also came from an upper-class black family. Her father was a minister who sent his daughter to the Tennessee Agricultural and Industrial University where she was educated to be a teacher (S140).

Together, Hansberry's parents created a household where the importance of education and serious social commitment were instilled in their children. Indeed, Hansberry's father ran unsuccessfully for Congress on the Republican ticket in 1940, and her mother worked as a ward committee person for the Republican party. To this, add a home which included a fine library containing world classics as well as works by and about black people (S87), and it is not surprising the well-to-do Hansberrys became cultural catalysts for black social life in Chicago.

In fact, frequent visitors included African-American artists and political leaders such as Paul Robeson, Duke Ellington, and Jesse Owens (S140) as well as Hansberry's uncle, William Leo Hansberry, a professor at Howard University and a prominent proponent of the study of African history and culture. He frequently brought some of his proud, foreign-born African students to her home, helping to provide a climate for the development of the future playwright's rich imagination as well as her social and racial sensitivities.

In 1938, in what was to become one of the most significant experiences the young Lorraine Hansberry was ever to have, her affluent father bought a larger home in a predominately white neighborhood, but in order to live there, he had to fight a civil rights case against segregationists all the way to the Supreme Court (S79). While he won the case, the threats of white homeowners (a brick thrown through their window almost hit Lorraine) made life intolerable. Embittered by his race's treatment at the hands of the white establishment, Carl Hansberry died in Mexico while making plans to move his family there (S140).

So while Hansberry was, as she was later to say in the autobiographical *To Be Young, Gifted and Black*, "born on the Southside of Chicago...black and female," she certainly had advantages and experiences that made her as much an outsider in the poor, black ghetto as she was a member, and this certainly had an effect on her artistic and psychological growth. For though neighbors appreciated her family's benevolence and social consciousness, they also considered the Hansberrys a wealthy clan somehow different from themselves.

It is not a wonder, then, that in her elementary school days, Hansberry was one who "listened and observed," perhaps, to some degree, because her fellow students grew up in conditions of abject poverty from which she was somewhat insulated (S87). In fact, once when she wore a new white fur coat to school, the poor children attacked her verbally and threw ink on her precious garment (S87). Such a painful incident helped shape her character, pushing her to confront the facts of ghetto life and to develop a strong sympathy for and understanding of the difficult lives her people led. Building bonds, if for no other reason than to survive socially, brought her in touch with the desperation and fierceness of a whole race of people ready to explode *like a raisin in the sun*. This awareness, combined with her family's dedication to the eradication of the injustice and prejudice that kept *all* classes of African-American people in the gutter, were important aspects of her early experience that would later be reformulated into the powerful social statements contained in her plays.

While in grade school, Hansberry earned only average grades in what she later referred to as an education in an inadequate "Jim Crow grade school system" (S140). Thus, she virtually educated herself by reading widely and listening to the thoughtful conversations involving politics, art, and culture regularly taking place in her home. In high school she continued to read avidly, excelling in English and history. And, of course, there was always her Uncle Leo Hansberry who inspired her interest in her African roots.

When it came time for college, Hansberry was admitted to the University of Wisconsin where she became the first black woman to live in her residence hall (S140). The university fostered her interest in liberal politics, civil rights, and social issues, and soon she became involved with the Young Progressives of America, of which she became president in 1949 (S140). However, her commitment to social justice was complimented by a growing interest in writing and the theater. She took a course in stage design and, for the first time, viewed plays by the likes of Ibsen, Strindberg and, most notably, a production of Sean O'Casey's *Juno and the Paycock* which, with its earthy sense of social awareness and class struggle, was to add to her perspective on how best to promote social justice. Perhaps the liberation of the oppressed could be accomplished with writing and with theater (S140).

In addition, Hansberry's interest in the humanities took her to the Art Institute of Chicago and to Guadalajara, Mexico, where she studied painting. Yet it was not time for her to commit herself to a life in the arts.

Becoming impatient with university life and her studies, in 1950 she moved to New York City with a craving for the *real*. In Harlem, she took a position on Paul Robeson's "radical" paper, *Freedom*, becoming its youngest staff member in 1950. She wrote news stories and reviews, conducted interviews and attended talks, her brilliant mind always embracing the flavor of the crowded, violent, vibrant life there. Not only was she initiated into political actualities of civil rights causes by the passionate Robeson, she also met and was influenced by many other important African-American writers and intellectuals, such as W.E.B. Du Bois and Langston Hughes (S140). Additionally, she began to develop a finer focus on the lives and politics of black people in other parts of America and throughout the world, in particular Africa with its burgeoning racial pride and revolutionary spirit (S87).

It is safe to say that in Hansberry's intellectual and emotional immersion in the plight of oppressed black people, this bright independent *woman in a man's world* began to feel acutely and empathize with the oppression of others in various social circumstances which placed them "outside" the prevailing majority, often making them victims of sexism and bigotry. In fact, herself a lesbian (S44, S95, S109, S122, S123, S125, S133, S147, S148), Hansberry wrote letters to lesbian and gay publications expressing her outrage at the sexism, bigotry, and homophobia that was as rampant in her own African-American community as it was in the society at large. In this regard, Robert Nemiroff (S128) has asserted that Hansberry's homosexuality "was not a peripheral or casual part of her life but contributed significantly on many levels to the sensitivity and complexity of her view of human beings and the world."

In short, Hansberry was growing into an articulate voice that spoke on behalf of any people who experienced the degradation of their lives due to discrimination, in whatever form it took and for whatever reason.

In 1952, while covering a picket line protesting discrimination in the athletic programs of New York University, Hansberry met her husband-to-be, and one-day producer of her plays, Robert Nemiroff, who was white and Jewish. From the time of their then unconventional white/black marriage in 1953, he enthusiastically shared her growing dedication to her writing. She quit her job with *Freedom* to devote more time to her literary endeavors, both she and her husband working a series of odd jobs to make ends meet while living in Greenwich Village (S128, S87).

For four years she struggled with her writing. In 1957, the

experiences of growing up on the Southside, her work at *Freedom*, her passionate sympathy for the oppressed, and her activist, social commitment to justice finally congealed in the first draft of a play about a black family in Chicago who, among other things, wanted to move from their cramped, kitchenette apartment into a larger house in a white neighborhood.

Taking its title from Langston Hughes' poem, *A Raisin in the Sun* was, initially, a "hard sell." Broadway producers were fearful of investing in a serious *Negro play* that might not appeal to the predominately white theater audience. Therefore, Hansberry and her associates raised the money for a traveling production which toured such cities as New Haven and Chicago to demonstrate its financial and artistic viability (S140). Their own enthusiasm for the play was shared by audience after audience, and finally this new, significant drama about a *real* black family opened at the Ethel Barrymore Theatre on March 11, 1959.

A Raisin in the Sun was an immediate success. Critics praised its realism, lauding how Hansberry set down, "without recourse to trickery or sentimentality the stresses and strains that torment a poor Negro family." The play contained "compassionate candor" (R8), with "flavorful" speech and an "infectious sense of [caustic] fun" (R10). Also of note was the cast of brilliant African-American actors under the direction of Lloyd Richards, the first black director on Broadway since the 1920s. They included Sidney Poitier, Claudia McNeil, Ruby Dee, Lou Gossett, Diana Sands, and Ossie Davis, who later replaced Poitier in the role of Walter (S140). Along with Hansberry's, their careers were launched with this play about the plight of black people trapped in ghetto life and ghetto consciousness who, nonetheless, longed to live the promise of the American dream, as had Hansberry and her own family.

A Raisin in the Sun ran for 530 performances and was destined for Hollywood. With the sale of the movie rights to Columbia pictures and the agreement that Hansberry would write the screenplay, the movie brought from Broadway McNeil, Poitier, Dee, Sands, and Gossett to recreate their roles for the screen. Most critics found that the play's "earthy drama and humor" (R49) were successfully translated into the 1961 film. Yet Hansberry was disappointed when some scenes she wished to add to sharpen the play's attack on racism and prejudice were scrapped by the producers. Also regrettable was the deletion of the original play's rendering of the relationship of African liberation and African-American civil rights movements by the character Asagai in the third act (S140).

A durable dramatic vehicle for which audiences seemed never to tire, Nemiroff and Charlotte Zaltzberg recreated the play into the Tony-Award-winning musical, *Raisin*, in 1973. It ran for 874 performances. And while this "redevelopment" of Hansberry's work de-emphasized much of the original drama's biting social comment in favor of the "flavor" of the black life of the Youngers put to music, it nonetheless contained, without the complexities of the drama, the story of the Younger family and the issues they, as blacks, faced in a white world (S128).

After continuous regional performances, *A Raisin in the Sun* was again produced for the Roundabout Theatre in New York in 1986, this time restoring those parts that had been cut from the original Broadway production (as well as the film version). The production was also presented on PBS's American Playhouse. Starring Danny Glover and Esther Rolle, it had the highest viewer ratings in the history of public television (S140).

By 1961, Hansberry's fame as a dramatist had established her as a major spokesperson for the cause of civil rights, and she continued to make many public statements and appearances on behalf of those who led oppressed lives. She also published widely on issues facing African-American artists and the theater, as well as on social issues and world affairs. The following titles suggest her range of interests and commitments: "American Theatre Needs Desegregating Too," "Black Revolution and the White Backlash," "Congolese Patriot," "The Legacy of W.E.B. Du Bois," "The Movement: Documentary of a Struggle for Equality," "Negroes and Africa," "Playwriting: Creative Constructiveness," "Thoughts on Genet, Mailer and the New Paternalism," and "This Complex of Womanhood." Yet all the while she was also working on a number of plays, one of which would become her next Broadway production.

The 1964 production of *The Sign in Sidney Brustein's Window* was, Hansberry said, to be an antidote to "the vogue of unmodified despair" in the works of such modern playwrights as Albee, Genet, and Beckett. Sidney's message is, as he says, "I care!" about life and the suffering of others (S140). Yet her audience was surprised to be greeted by a play set, not in a black ghetto, but rather in Greenwich Village with a Jewish intellectual for a protagonist. It was an unsentimental drama about ideas and the complexities of human relationships and social commitment with an array of characters (including a homosexual, for instance) who happened, for the most part, *not* to be black. Because of these factors, as well as the fact that Hansberry was suffering from terminal cancer at the time of the play's production which made it difficult for her to help work it into a satisfying whole, the drama (as well as a 1972 revival with music) was not generally well-received by the New York critics (S140, S87).

In spite of a fine cast, including Rita Moreno, Gabriel Dell and Alice Ghostly, many critics found *The Sign in Sidney Brustein's Window* uneven. While they sometimes admired and regretted what appeared to be Hansberry's didactic social statements, the play was deemed "labored and long, inefficiently focused, and unable to stir much sympathetic or empathic feelings in the audience" (R66). However, some found the drama a triumph which "successfully reached into the turbulence of contemporary New York life" by a playwright who had shown herself not merely to be a "one-shot author" (R69).

Because of the uneven reviews, *The Sign in Sidney Brustein's Window* struggled to survive. It did, however, run for one hundred and one performances, mainly because of the sacrifice and efforts of those who made keeping a serious play on Broadway open a *cause* (S79). Some actors gave up part of their salaries; others made donations and campaigned for the production. In spite of all the support it had, though, *The Sign in Sidney Brustein's Window* finally closed the day Hansberry died from cancer on January 12, 1965 (S14).

Remarkably, however, Hansberry's death did not mark the end of her career as a dramatist. Her former husband Robert Nemiroff (they had secretly divorced months before her death) was designated her literary executor and proceeded to pull together and produce plays based upon her *works in progress* and her other writings. Already mentioned was his 1973 production of the musical *Raisin*, based on her celebrated play. But before that, responding to a New York radio station's request for a commemoration of the second anniversary of her death, he adapted some of her published and unpublished writings under the title *To Be Young, Gifted and Black*, a phrase coined by Hansberry herself (S79).

In 1969 *To Be Young, Gifted and Black* became the longest-running off-Broadway play in the 1968-69 season (380 performances) and continued with successful tours around the country. Such actors as Cicely Tyson, Moses Gunn, Barbara Baxley, Claudia McNeil, Ruby Dee, Blythe Danner, and Roy Scheider were featured in some of the casts of this montage of scenes focusing on various facets and nuances of African-

American life, Hansberry's in particular (S87). The play, which Nemiroff called "the portrait of an individual, the workbook of an artist, and the chronicle of a rebel who celebrated the human spirit," was made into a film for educational television in January of 1972.

The next posthumous production of Hansberry's work was *Les Blancs*, a play focusing on continental African struggles for liberation. She had begun it in 1960 and worked on it until her death. Again, Nemiroff took what she had left behind and, with some reworking, produced it at the Longacre Theatre on November 15, 1970 (S79).

Les Blancs is notable as a work by the first African-American playwright to dramatize the revolutionary struggle for black liberation in contemporary Africa. Hansberry wrote the play, starring James Earl Jones and Cameron Mitchell, as a response to Jean Genet's *Les Negres* (*The Blacks*, 1960) which she criticized for its poor portrayal of its characters as believable human beings. Her drama is one of ideas, most of it dealing with the political and moral issues expressed in the serious conversations of her characters (S79).

While some critics found *Les Blancs*, which Hansberry thought might be her most important play (S79), to be first rate, others found it to be a weak, didactic confab by Nemiroff and his associates, and one which seemed to endorse violent, black revolt against whites (S140). It closed after only forty performances.

Hansberry left two other completed plays, both published in 1972, which were never professionally produced in New York: *The Drinking Gourd* and *What Use Are Flowers*. *The Drinking Gourd* was written in 1960 for NBC television as one of a series of dramas commemorating the Civil War centennial. Set in the pre-Civil War South, it is a stark drama-tization of slavery's effects on *both* white and black people. Yet even while such luminaries as Claudia McNeil, Fredric March, and Florence Eldridge had agreed to act in the Dore Schary production, network executives finally killed it, partly because Hansberry's script treated white characters as much victims of the system of slavery as were the blacks (S79). In short, the unromanticized, and thereby disturbing depiction of the slave/master society, was blocked because of a 1960s sense of "paternalism" that sought to guard the white and black viewing public from a rendering of anything so complex as what the *actual* experience of slavery was.

What Use Are Flowers, finally produced in Atlanta at the 14th Street Playhouse as part of the National Black Arts Festival on July 30,

1994, is a fantasy-like allegory focusing on life after a nuclear holocaust has destroyed all civilization. A wise, old man tries to instill the virtues of civilization and culture as he knows them into a handful of children who have also survived. And although the children demonstrate some of the same jealous, self destructive impulses of their parents, they nonetheless have the instinct to cooperate and build. Nemiroff (S79) notes that the play was Hansberry's answer to Beckett's sense of absurdity and hopelessness in *Waiting For Godot* (1952). In it she expresses an optimistic, though guarded, humanism (S79).

A portion of another play entitled "*Toussaint*: Excerpt From Act I of a Work in Progress," is an unfinished manuscript about the Haitian hero, Toussaint L'Ouverture, whom Hansberry had admired since childhood. At one time conceived by the playwright as an opera, the published scene from *Toussaint*, like *A Raisin in the Sun* and *The Drinking Gourd*, delves into the devastating effects of racism and poverty, as well as the resilience of the human spirit, this time in Haiti of the 1780s. The excerpt reveals a sophisticated exploration of various levels of slavery, and how the institution oppresses both white and black. While produced professionally only once for a 1961 educational television program entitled "Playwrights at Work," the scene's director, Lloyd Richards noted its quality, commenting that the scene was so well-written, it could have gone into rehearsal almost at once with very little change (S140).

Finally, when reviewing Lorraine Hansberry's short, brilliant career as a dramatist, one can only speculate where, had she lived longer, her intelligence, wit, social commitment, and dazzling artistry would have led. Suffice to say, literary and cultural critics are now *re-reading* her works in light of the civil rights movements of the 70s, 80s, and 90s, issues of gender, the feminist movement, and sexuality, as well as concerns pertaining to the structure and health of the family and its ramifications in our society. In these and other areas, Hansberry's observations and vision display remarkable foresight and universal relevance, and her work continues to be well worth study and admiration.

The Plays:
Summaries, Productions,
and Critical Overviews

The following is a chronologically arranged collection of summaries, production credits, and critical overviews of Hansberry's published theatrical work. The summaries provide outlines of the dramatic action of each play. The professional credits corresponding to the major productions (both stage and film) identify producers, directors, casts, lengths of runs, etc. (The plays lacking production credits were never professionally produced, or only received minor runs.) A list of reviews and other relevant secondary citations follows the production information. The overviews trace the plays' and films' histories and critical receptions. Citations are keyed to the appropriate entries in the Secondary Bibliographies of this volume. ("P" numbers refer to primary bibliography.)

A RAISIN IN THE SUN (1959). P5

   The Characters -- LENA YOUNGER, the matriarch of the Younger family whose strong will, compassion, and religious convictions help her act as the family's head until the day her son can; WALTER LEE YOUNGER, Lena's son, in his thirties, who is a chauffeur but longs to be financially independent and his own boss; BENEATHA YOUNGER, Walter's intellectual sister who is a college student planning to go to medical school; RUTH YOUNGER, the wife of Walter who, like her husband, longs for a better life for their son; TRAVIS YOUNGER, Walter and Ruth's ten-year-old son; JOSEPH ASAGAI, a college student from Nigeria and friend of Beneatha's; GEORGE MURCHISON, a wealthy college student and friend of Beneatha's; KARL LINDER, the only white character in the play who represents the white community which doesn't want the Youngers to move into their neighborhood; MRS. JOHNSON, the Younger's neighbor; BOBO and WILLY, two friends of Walter; TWO MOVING MEN.

Plot Summary -- (Based on the 25th Anniversary Stage Production text (P5) which includes portions of the play deleted from the original 1959 stage production and the 1961 film version). Act I, Scene 1: The scene opens on a weary living room of the Younger's apartment on Chicago's Southside, sometime between World War II and the present. It is seven thirty in the morning, and Ruth, still youthful but disappointed in what life had given her, awakens her sluggish son who is sleeping on a make-down bed in the center of the room. He reluctantly rises and goes down the hall to the bathroom the family shares with other tenants. She then rouses her husband and starts preparing breakfast. They bicker a bit, Ruth expressing irritation at Walter's having kept the family up late the night before while he and his friends talked. Wanting to smooth things over, he remarks how young she looks at that moment and complains when she rejects his gestures of affection. Travis returns from the bathroom and Walter heads for it. As Travis eats his breakfast, he asks his mother for fifty cents. She harshly informs the boy they don't have the money and tells him he may have only enough for his lunch. Becoming gentle, she coaxes her angry son into giving her a good-bye kiss. When Walter returns and hears that she had told the boy they couldn't afford to give him the fifty cents, he pridefully defies his wife, as if to prove something to his son and her, and gives the departing, gleeful boy a dollar. Then he begins to tell his wife of his hopes about going into business for himself by buying a liquor store with his friends. He wants her to convince his mother to give him the money he needs to pay off the proper people and to invest in the store. He is irritated at Ruth's lack of interest in and cynical attitude toward a dream he is desperate to make come true. He decries her for being a "colored" woman who does not take seriously his manly yearnings to achieve something substantial for himself and his family. Beneatha enters the room and, noting the bathroom is in use, sits down to read the paper while Walter quizzes her on her commitment to become a doctor. They bicker over what their mother should do with their late father's insurance money, which is due to arrive shortly. Knowing that Walter has plans for the money, Beneatha proclaims that it is their mother's to spend the way she wishes, and that she doesn't expect any for her schooling. Walter flares at her seeming arrogance and points out the sacrifices the rest of the family has made for her to go to school. He suggests she does not need to be a doctor, only a nurse or a wife like other women. Beneatha again reiterates that the money is their mother's to do with as she wishes, but that she is glad an investment in a liquor store is unlikely. Walter, after having to get some carfare from his wife, angrily leaves for work. Mama, a woman in her early sixties, "full-bodied and strong," enters, looks at her peaked potted plant in the window, and wonders who has been slamming doors so early in the morning. Ruth reports that Walter and Beneatha had been fighting again. Though insisting that she's not meddling, she picks at Ruth, suggesting that she needs to give her son a hot breakfast and not cold cereal. Ruth asks Mama what she plans to do with the insurance money, and she tells Mama that Walter needs his chance, even if it is selling liquor. Mama tells the exhausted Ruth that she should stay home from work (in a white household) today, that a check for ten thousand dollars is coming and not to worry about the money she would lose. Mama enjoys Ruth's suggestion that she take a trip with the money. But Mama says that some of it is to go for Beneatha's education and that, perhaps, the rest could be a down payment on a house for the family. Mama reminisces about her dead husband, recalling how he loved his children, how he dreamed of making their lives better, but how impossible it was for a black man to accomplish his dreams. Beneatha returns with the news that she will be taking guitar lessons and, with Mama's question as to why she takes up so many different things, proclaims she experiments with different forms of self-expression. Mama and Ruth laugh at this and quiz her about her plans to go out with George Murchison that evening, wondering why she doesn't really like this rich boy. Beneatha says she finds him shallow and asserts that rich "colored" people are more snobbish than rich white people, and consequently wouldn't want her, a poor girl, marrying into their family. She gets angry and says her first priority is to become a doctor. And responding to her mother's reply of "God willing," proclaims that God has nothing to do with it--that He is just an idea--that there is no God at all. Mama, asserting her authority as head of the household, slaps Beneatha and forces her to repeat, "In my mother's house there is still God." Mama leaves the room, and the humbled, though proud, Beneatha leaves, resenting her mother's tyranny. Mama returns lamenting that she no longer seems to understand her children. Ruth consoles her as she looks to her potted plant, the only garden she has ever had. When Mama turns around, she sees that Ruth has fainted.

Act I, Scene 2: It is the following morning, Saturday, and Mama and Beneatha are cleaning house. Mama tells Travis that his mother has gone to take care of some business. Beneatha answers the phone and gives it to Walter so he can speak to Willie Harris, his friend and investment partner. Mama and Beneatha banter about the roaches Beneatha is spraying for, and Mama tells her that Ruth has gone to the doctor. Without saying, they both suspect pregnancy. Beneatha then gets a call from Joseph Asagai, an African boy and "intellectual," whom she invites to the house. She warns her offended mother not to ask silly questions of him and tells her that his people are more in need of salvation from the British and French than they are from heathenism, for which Mama donates at church. Ruth enters, and everybody obviously recognizes that she's going to have a baby. Beneatha asks if Ruth "planned" the baby, to Mama's irritation. They call down to tell Travis, who is chasing a rat, to come upstairs. He does, and after describing the bloody event, is sent back out. Mama begins to worry about Ruth's demeanor. She takes Ruth to lie down and Beneatha, visibly disturbed, answers the door and welcomes Asagai. The sophisticated young man gives her a present of Nigerian robes and records which she happily accepts. He shows her how to wear the robes and tells her she needs to let her hair be as natural as his. He accuses her, in altering the natural form of her hair, of being an "assimilationist." She denies this and expresses her resentment of what she senses is the nature of his affection for her, suggesting that the sort of romance he envisions is the sort found in the novels *men* write. She demands something more than that, and he mocks the notion of "liberated" women. Mama enters and puts on the charm, inviting him to return for a home-cooked meal. He tells them that his nickname for Beneatha means "One for Whom Bread--Food--Is Not Enough," and Beneatha appreciates this. After he leaves, Mama notes how handsome he is and Beneatha, admiring the robes, gets her raincoat and leaves after him. Ruth enters, and the mail comes with the anticipated ten thousand dollars. They open the letter and admire the check, but Mama is strangely unhappy. She asks Ruth where she went today, and Ruth tells her she went to the doctor, but Mama, picking up on Ruth's earlier slip of the tongue, knows that she went to the woman who performs abortions. At this moment, Walter bounds in asking about the money. Mama tells him to talk to his wife and that there will be no investment in a liquor store. Walter reminds them of their paltry living conditions and prepares to leave in disappointment. He and Ruth have words and Mama insists that he sit down and be civil. With Ruth in the other room, Mama asks her son what is bothering him so. She councils him that the liquor store is a bad idea. He desperately tells her how important the money is to him, how he wants so many things for his family. She recounts his humble blessings, but he mocks his life and his menial job, saying he must make some money and something of himself or he'll have no self respect at all. He says money, not freedom, is life, to which Mama repeats that she does not understand her children and their values anymore. She shocks him with news that Ruth is expecting a baby, and that she's thinking about an abortion. Ruth confirms this, and Walter leaves, refusing to do as his mother says and tell Ruth that an abortion is out of the question. Mama calls him a disgrace to his father's memory and asks for her hat.

Act II, Scene 1: Later the same day, Ruth is ironing, and Beneatha comes out of her room dressed in her Nigerian costume. She begins to dance to a lovely Nigerian melody. Walter, who has been drinking, enters and watches his sister. Joining in the dance, he pulls his shirt open and gestures with an imaginary spear, and both celebrate their African roots to the rhythm of the music. Ruth shuts off the music and opens the door to let George

Murchison enter as she scolds Beneatha and her husband. When George tells Beneatha to change for their date, she pulls off her headdress to reveal her close-cropped, unstraightened hair. All are shocked as Beneatha proclaims that she hates "assimilationist" Negroes. They mock her concern for African culture. She goes to change, and Ruth and Walter chat with George, Walter asking him with resentment why college boys wear "faggoty-looking" white shoes. Walter continues to express his jealousy and resentment for the well-to-do George as Ruth tries to quell him. He says no one is for him and everyone is against him, even his mother. When Beneatha comes in, George gets ready to leave with her. Walter says he likes Beneatha's new hair style. As they leave, George cynically refers to Walter as *Prometheus*, which Walter doesn't understand. Walter says he's trapped in a race of people who don't know how to do anything but moan, pray, and have babies. Ruth says that she's sorry about her pregnancy and that maybe she should go through with her plans to eliminate it. Ruth tries to get him to talk to her, and he calms down and begins to, wondering why they've lost what they once had together. Mama then returns and answers their inquiries as to where she's been, saying that she was downtown tending to some business. Travis enters and Ruth commences to scold him for his lateness when Mama interrupts because she wants Travis to be the first to know something; she's bought a house. Ruth is as pleased as Walter is stunned as Mama describes the house bought with the insurance money. They are shocked, however, when she mentions the address. Ruth and Walter recognize immediately that it is located in a white neighborhood. Yet Ruth is desperate to leave the cramped apartment and relishes the thought of the house. Mama tells Walter that she bought the house because she had seen her family falling apart. She asks Walter to say she did the right thing. He refuses, remarking cruelly that *she* is the head of the family--*she* runs their lives as she sees fit. He then tells her bitterly that she has butchered up his dream.

Act II, Scene 2: A few weeks later, there are some packing crates in the living room. George and Beneatha return from a date, and he tells her he wants a nice girl to go out with, not one who wants to talk about ideas. She says good night to him as Mama enters. She tells her mother that George is a fool, and

Mama says, if that's the case, she shouldn't waste her time with him. Beneatha is pleased with this response. As she leaves, Ruth enters and suggests to Mama that Walter is again drunk and sleeping. Mrs. Johnson enters expressing happiness for the Youngers' good fortune. A nasty gossip, she tells them of a newspaper report of a black family that was bombed out of their house by whites, and she goes on to say that the Youngers' names might be in the paper for the same reason one day. She slyly criticizes Beneatha for thinking she's too good for people who aren't college-educated, and then says that Walter has nothing to be ashamed about being a chauffeur. To this Mama responds, saying that her husband was right; people shouldn't be others' servants. Mrs. Johnson leaves and the phone rings with the message that if Walter doesn't appear for work the next day, he'll lose his job. He's just entered the room, and Ruth says that she was told he had not been to work for three days. He doesn't care about that nor about the prospect of losing his job. He tells his wife and mother that he's been driving and wandering aimlessly the last few days, ending up at a bar. Mama is very upset at this, and she says she's been wrong. She gives him an envelope with sixty five hundred dollars in it, the insurance money left over after the thirty five hundred dollar down payment on the house. She tells him that her children are her only concern, and that he's to put three thousand dollars of what remains in a savings account for Beneatha's medical schooling and the rest in a checking account of his own. He may do with his share what he wishes. Walter is amazed at his mother's trust and love. When his son enters, Walter tells him that their lives are going to change due to a transaction he is going to make tonight. Walter says in a few years he'll have an office, secretaries, and a car. Ruth will have a fine car, too, and Travis, he says with excitement which, in turn, excites the boy, will be able to attend the college of his choice and be whatever he wants in life.

Act II, Scene 3: One week later, it's Saturday and moving day. Beneatha and Ruth are doing some final packing and clearly relishing the move. Ruth says that she and Walter went to the movies last night and held hands, something they haven't done in ages. A deeply happy Walter comes in and puts on a record, the music of which he and Ruth begin to dance to. Beneatha calls them old-fashioned, and Walter teases her about being one of those "New Negroes" who are too serious about race and civil rights. The doorbell sounds and Beneatha lets in a middle-aged white man who asks for Lena Younger. Karl Linder introduces himself to Walter, who says he handles most of his mother's business matters. Linder explains that he represents the Clybourne Park Improvement Association which, among other things, welcomes new people, like the Youngers, to their community and also handles "special community problems." Beneatha senses what his mission is. As he proceeds to say that it's best to talk things out, and that race prejudice has nothing to do with it, he gradually works up to the point that his neighborhood is for whites only. He says that the Association is willing to buy the house back from them for more than they paid. Walter, who is getting more and more upset, finally tells him to get out. Linder leaves his card on the table and goes. Mama and Travis enter. Mama is told she had a visitor and, in the conversation, gradually understands what the caller wanted. She wonders if Linder threatened the family. Mama begins to fuss with her plant, and the family takes this opportunity to give her gifts they have secretly bought for her: gardening tools and a hat. As they begin to pack again, the doorbell rings and Bobo is there with the message that Willy has taken Walter's money and left town. Walter wilts in sorrow at the news, and Mama gets him to confess that all the money she had given him, including Beneatha's share, is lost. Mama speaks of her late husband's sacrifices and despairs that her son has lost such hard-earned money so quickly. She then, tempted to strike Walter, stops and asks God for strength.

Act III, Scene 1: It is an hour later. Walter is lying down and Beneatha sits in profound disappointment. Asagai arrives to help with the move. She tells him that her brother has lost the insurance money. She recounts sadly how she became interested in becoming a doctor to cure people. Her idealism shattered, she questions Asagai's hopes for an Africa "cured" of colonialism. Even if independence is gained, she pessimistically asks, what about all the crooks who will plunder the new countries? Asagai says she should not let money that was not hers anyway ruin her ideals and ambitions for her people. He then asks her to return to Nigeria with him. He leaves her to think it over as Walter rises and enters the room. Beneatha berates him angrily as he fever-ishly looks for and finds a piece of paper on the table and rushes out. Mama enters sadly, her hopes crushed. She tells the women that they won't be moving now. Ruth pleads with her to make the move, but Mama suggests with resignation that they might just as well fix the apartment up and give up trying to do too much. Walter returns and says he's called and told "The Man," Linder, to come right over. He says cynically that he's no longer going to be one of "the tooken," that he's going to start taking instead. His mother despairs at what she hears him say, and tells him that their people, even when they were slaves, were not "dead inside." Walter tells them what he's going to say to Linder when he makes the deal, taking on the persona of a slow-witted movie stereotype of a Negro. Hating what he's going to do, he breaks down and goes into the bedroom. When Beneatha remarks that Walter is no longer her brother, Mama comes to his defense, saying that he needs love now more than ever. The moving men arrive down-stairs, and Linder is at the door. Mama insists Walter let his son watch him do the disgraceful thing he's about to do. In a broken speech, he tells Linder that the Youngers come from generations of proud people, finally stating that they will move into the house their father earned for them. When Linder appeals to Mama, she says her son has spoken, and they will move. He leaves, and Mama gets the family busy with the loading. Beneatha says that Asagai has asked her to marry him, and she and Walter begin to argue over it as they leave. Mama smiles and says Walter finally came into his manhood, and Ruth agrees. Left alone in the room, Mama silently, though emotionally, surveys the place she has lived in for so long. Beginning to go, she remembers and returns to get her potted plant and then leaves the room for the last time.

Productions and Credits -- Broadway: Ethel Barrymore Theatre, New York City, March 11, 1959. (Moved to Belasco Theatre on October 19, 1959.) 530 performances. Winner of the New York Drama Critics Award for best play of 1959.

> Producers: Philip Rose and David J. Cogan
> Director: Lloyd Richards
> Set Design: Ralph Alswang
> Lighting: Ralph Alswang

Costumes: Virginia Volland
Cast: Walter Lee Younger -- Sidney Poitier
      (succeeded by Ossie Davis)
    Mama Lena Younger -- Claudia McNeil
      (succeeded by Francis Williams)
    Ruth Younger -- Ruby Dee
    Beneatha Younger -- Diana Sands
    Joseph Asagai -- Ivan Dixon
      (succeeded by Edward Hall)
    Karl Linder -- John Fiedler
    George Murchison -- Louis Gossett
    Travis Younger -- Glynn Turman
      (succeeded by Charles Richardson)
    Bobo -- Lonne Elder III
    Moving Men -- Ed Hall (succeeded by Lincoln Kilpatrick), Douglas Turner

Film: Columbia Pictures, March 29, 1961. Black and white, 35 mm, 128 minutes.
Producers: David Susskind, Phillip Rose
Director: Daniel Petrie
Screenplay: Lorraine Hansberry
Photography: Charles Lawton (Location scenes filmed in Chicago)
Art Director: Carl Anderson
Film Editors: William A. Lyon, Paul Weatherwax
Music: Laurence Rosenthal
Orchestrations: Arthur Morton
Cast: Walter Lee Younger -- Sidney Poitier
    Mama Lena Younger -- Claudia McNeil
    Ruth Younger -- Ruby Dee
    Beneatha Younger -- Diana Sands
    Joseph Asagai -- Ivan Dixon
    Linder -- John Fiedler
    George Murchison -- Louis Gossett
    Travis Younger -- Stephen Perry
    Bobo -- Joel Fluellen
    Willie -- Roy Glenn
    Bartender -- Ray Stubbs

Taxi Driver -- Rudolph Monroe
Employer -- George DeNormand
Herman -- Louis Terkel
Chauffeur -- Thomas D. Jones

"25th Anniversary Revival": Roundabout Theatre, New York City, August 1986.

Producers: The Roundabout Theatre Company (Gene Feist and Todd Haimes) and Robert Nemiroff
Director: Harold Scott
Set: Thomas Cariello
Lighting: Shirley Prendergast
Costumes: Judy Dearing
Cast: Walter Lee Younger -- James Pickens Jr.
Mama Lena Younger -- Olivia Cole
Ruth Younger -- Starletta DuPois
Beneatha Younger -- Kim Yancey
Joseph Asagai -- Vondie Curtis-Hall
Karl Linder -- John Fiedler
George Murchison -- Joseph C. Phillips
Bobo -- Stephen Henderson
others

American Playhouse Television Presentation based upon the "25th Anniversary Stage Production" directed by Harold Scott. Broadcast February 1, 1989.

Producers: Chiz Schultz, Robert Nemiroff, Jaki Brown, Toni Livingston, Josephine Abady Productions, Fireside Entertainment Corporation, and KCET/Los Angeles in association with WNET/New York
Director: Bill Duke
Production Design: Thomas Cariello
Lighting Design: Bill Klages
Costume Design: Celia Bryant and Judy Dearing
Music: Ed Bland
Editor: Gary Anderson
Cameras: Greg Cook, Gregory Harms, Kenneth A. Patterson
Cast: Walter Lee Younger -- Danny Glover
Mama Lena Younger -- Esther Rolle

Ruth Younger -- Starletta DuPois
Beneatha Younger -- Kim Yancey
Joseph Asagai -- Lou Ferguson
Karl Linder -- John Fiedler
George Murchison -- Joseph C. Phillips
Travis Younger -- Kimble Joyner
Bobo -- Stephen Henderson
Mrs. Johnson -- Helen Martin
Moving Men -- Ron O.J. Parson, Charles Watts

RAISIN (musical)

Productions and Credits -- Broadway: 46th Street Theatre, New York City, October 18, 1973. (Moved to the Lunt-Fontanne Theatre, January 14, 1975.) 847 performances. Winner of the 1974 "Tonys" for Best Musical and Best Actress (Virginia Capers).

Producer: Robert Nemiroff
Director/Choreographer: Donald McKayle
Book: Robert Nemiroff and Charlotte Zaltzberg
Music: Judd Woldin
Lyrics: Robert Brittan
Scenery: Robert U. Taylor
Costumes: Bernard Johnson
Lighting: William Mintzer
Musical Director/Conductor: Howard A. Roberts
Orchestrations: Al Cohn and Robert Freedman
Vocal Arrangements: Joyce Brown and Howard A. Roberts
Dance Arrangements: Judd Woldin
Original Cast Album: CBS Records
Cast: Walter Lee Younger -- Joe Morton
Mama Lena Younger -- Virginia Capers
Ruth Younger -- Ernestine Jackson
Beneatha Younger -- Deborah Allen
Joseph Asagai -- Robert Jackson
Karl Linder -- Richard Sanders (also played by Will Mott)
Travis Younger -- Ralph Carter (also played by Paul Carrington)

> Mrs. Johnson -- Helen Martin
> Bobo Jones -- Ted Ross
> Willy Harris -- Walter P. Brown
> Pastor -- Herb Downer
> Pastor's Wife -- Marenda Perry
> Bar Girl -- Elaine Beener
> Pusher -- Al Perryman
> Victim -- Loretta Abbott
> African Drummer -- Cheif Bey
> People of the Southside -- Chuck Thorpes, Eugene Little, Karen Burke, Zelda Pulliam, Elaine Beener, Renee Rose, Paul Carrington, Marenda Perry, Gloria Turner, Don Jay, Glenn Brooks, Marilyn Hamilton

Reviews (play) -- R1-R48; (film) -- R49-R62; (musical) -- R133-R150.

Other Secondary Sources -- S2, S3, S4, S5, S9, S11, S12, S13, S14, S15, S17, S18, S19, S20, S21, S22, S23, S24, S25, S26, S30, S32, S35, S36, S37, S38, S39, S40, S41, S42, S43, S47, S48, S53, S54, S60, S63, S65, S67, S68, S69, S70, S71, S72, S79, S80, S81, S83, S87, S88, S89, S92, S94, S96, S97, S99, S100, S101, S102, S103, S104, S106, S107, S108, S109, S111, S113, S115, S118, S119, S124, S126, S127, S128, S129, S130, S131, S132, S135, S137, S139, S140, S143, S144, S146, S149.

Critical Overview -- The March 11, 1959 opening on Broadway of *A Raisin in the Sun* brought immediate fame to the 29-year-old Lorraine Hansberry. Her play was awarded the New York Drama Critics Circle Award over Eugene O'Neill's *A Touch of the Poet*, Tennessee Williams' *Sweet Bird of Youth*, and Archibald MacLeish's *J.B.* And while some then suggested that her play won the award because of a liberal bias, since that time critics have come to view the drama as a classic, one that changed the landscape of the American theater forever by spotlighting issues of racial injustice, the changing status of women, sexism, African independence, and colonialism--all in a passionate, realistic portrayal of black family life (S128).

But how did Hansberry's play accomplish this revolution, and
what did audiences take away from the play? A survey of scholarly work on the drama reveals the scope of reactions. Carter
cites critics who feel *A Raisin in the Sun* intended to "convince
whites that blacks were exactly like them," and to demonstrate
that integration was the key to the elimination of racial injustice.
In part, this reading was based on a remark Hansberry made in an
interview in which she asserted that hers was not merely a "*Negro
play*, it was about honest-to-God, believable, many-sided people
who happened to be Negroes" (S128). This led some to praise the
drama for its "universal" vision, one that moves beyond mere
concerns with white and black to a hope for unity and survival not
unlike that found in Miller's *Death of a Salesman*, where the
family provides a medium for the playwright to probe the modern
existential condition and to argue for human sympathy and understanding.

However, literary critics like McKelly (S139) note that the
reason *A Raisin in the Sun* was accepted with such enthusiasm
was because it "posed no threat" to the dominant, white American
culture. For McKelly, Walter Lee is no Willy Loman; he is a
character who has sinned against the "universally-held, and hence
universally-applauded, American imperatives of honesty and
dignity which the author promotes as sacred." McKelly goes on
to claim that even the "would-be radical Beneatha," never "strays
far from the well-worn path of middle class upward mobility." In
this vein, Guttmann (S42) finds that the play contains a "quieter
sort of protest" against racism than those by LeRoi Jones, for instance, with their expression of a black rage that questions the
hopes of those, like Hansberry, who are exponents of racial integration as a panacea for racial injustice. Keyssar (S80), too,
while admitting to the complexities of Hansberry's work, insists
that her play is for white audiences and is written so as to allow
whites to "leave the theater happily persuaded that still another
family has rightfully joined the infinitely extensive American
middle class." Unfortunately, Keyssar (S115) concludes, in *A
Raisin in the Sun*, Hansberry "constructed a dramatic world in
which the wit and charm of the characters distracted the audience
from the danger and contradictions of the social world they in-
habited..."

Adams (S26) also criticizes the play for seeming to say the "correct societal-familial value-system, a value system passed down from Big Walter through Lena...is White." He goes on to assert that it is clear "what occurs on the conscious, social level (Walter's becoming mature, responsible, and normal)" is his adoption of this [white] value system. Taking the very title of the drama to task, Adam notes that, ironically, Walter and the family's dream is "not deferred" indefinitely, as the epigraph to the play might suggest. At the conclusion of *A Raisin in the Sun*, the Youngers are not about "to explode" in rebellion against "oppressive white power." Rather, buying a home, they are taking a first step in achieving the American dream just as Hansberry's father had with his banking and real estate investment ventures.

Yet such critics often ignore aspects of *A Raisin in the Sun* that render more complex the issues the play addresses. It should not be forgotten Hansberry's father, himself, failed to move his family into a white neighborhood due to the ingrained racism and violence of white, bigoted society, and, therefore, was on the verge of taking them to Mexico to live at the time of his death. And the play expresses vividly this disillusionment with the promise of the "American dream" on the part of African-Americans as well as Hansberry's own "anti-assimilationist viewpoint" in the characters of Beneatha and Asagai, she in her refusal to give up her fight against the racism and sexism which would keep her from becoming a doctor for her people, and both for their vision of an Africa free of the colonial yoke that has characterized the intolerable oppression of black people, both in Africa and America (S2). Furthermore, in recognizing the play's successful portrayal of the complexities of a real black family festering in poverty, Ossie Davis (S9) wrote that Hansberry well knew "that the American dream held by Mama is as unworkable in this day and age as that held by Walter. She knew that Mama's old-fashioned morality was no solution to being poor and being black in America, even in the suburbs." Brown (S38) agrees, noting how critics of Hansberry, such as Harold Cruse and C.W.E. Bigsby, miss the playwright's irony and ambiguity in her dramatic critique of the American propensity to "confuse material achievement with the total promise of the American dream." Indeed, as Ward (S71)

puts it, those who find Walter Lee a "repository of all the negative, materialistic aspirations of American society," hold a
"tremendously simplistic" view of the character and the play. He
is a complex "bearer of aims and goals that have been conditioned
by the prevailing values of society..." He is "flawed, contradictory, irascible, impulsive, furious...desperate," and ready to explode.

More contemporary literary critics have observed, along with
Greenfield (S83), *A Raisin in the Sun*'s important exploration
into the complexity of African-American society and family life.
In this regard, the play "examines differences between older rural
blacks and younger urban blacks, the tensions between educated
and uneducated blacks," while presenting a "credible picture of a
crisis in self-image among black males..." Moreover, in her examination of feminism in twentieth century women's drama,
Friedman (S88) suggests that Mama is not a dramatization of
black women who emasculate black men. Rather, she is a mother
who repudiates the "negative images of black women as passive
and/or destructive," and is a woman who contributes to the survival of her family and community, sometimes with an "active
resistance often necessary to that survival." In discussing Hansberry's commitment to a feminist perspective, Carter (S94) asserts that Hansberry saw her male characters as caught in the
same cultural web of "male supremacy" as her females, and
dramatized the "resulting harm they do to women and themselves."

Keppel (S146) investigates *A Raisin in the Sun* as a "social
document of unappreciated political radicalism and thematic
complexity," and seeks to reclaim the "text from those who had
celebrated it as an affirmation of the American dream." And
Parks (S149) identifies the newest version of the play, which
contains restored passages of what had been cut from the
Broadway and film productions, as one which places the drama
"back at the center of black women's concerns for the continuity
of the culture and survival of the self and family," issues at the
heart of "black feminist theatre." Along these lines, Berrian
(S104) focuses on the play's theme of cross-cultural marriage in
the characters of Asagai, which she sees as a "testimony of self-
affirmation, new freedom and a positive step towards black

identity," while Nemiroff (S106), in his foreword to the unabridged edition, celebrates the play's emphasis on "women's con-sciousness," the "revolutionary ferment in Africa," "the value systems of the black family and the conflict between generations, concepts of African American beauty, identity, hairstyle," and the "relationships" of husbands, wives, black men, and black women.

A survey of theatrical reviews of *A Raisin in the Sun* in its various forms reveals some of the concerns of the scholarly writers as well as a perspective on the dramatic qualities of the play. By in large, they were positive:

Atkinson (R3) observed that *A Raisin in the Sun* resembled Chekhov's *The Cherry Orchard* in its "knowledge of how character is controlled by environment" and its "alternation of humor and pathos." Along with Aston (R2), he applauded the play as one that did not try "to prove one thing or another" but to tell "the inner as well as the outer truth about a Negro family." Tynan (R9) compared Hansberry's to yet another playwright's work saying that, while it was not without its sentimentality, it generated the same kind of sympathy for its characters as Clifford Odets' *Awake and Sing* had 24 years before. The *Time* reviewer (R10) agreed, remarking that *A Raisin in the Sun* might be "somber, or merely sentimental, if its milieu were not so sharply objective, its speech so flavorful, and its infectious sense of fun so caustic."

Hewes (R15) appreciated *A Raisin in the Sun*'s being about "real people" who only happen to be "colored people," noting their "inner family joys and anxieties" were universal ones. Hayes (R17) also liked the universal scope of the play, admiring in Hansberry's work the same "poetry of concern" found in the novels of Theodore Dreiser. Noting a similarity of her play with those of Sean O'Casey, the "playwright of Dublin slum-dwellers," Arnow (R28) spoke of how Hansberry's characters grow in stature "as they grope their way up their Everest of moral predicaments," leaving the audience "with a dazzling vision of the modern situation of mankind." And Lewis (R29) liked the play because of its lack of "Freudian" implications, "cynical motivations," and "symbolism." Written in the naturalistic manner, it is a "straight forward social drama...refreshing in its simplicity."

As did many, Watts (R8) applauded the "excellent acting" in

the first Broadway production of *A Raisin in the Sun*. Yet Brein (R26) insisted that while the play dealt with important social issues, the "Negroes on stage are stage Negroes...stock Samuel French types," and he chided the overacting by some performers. Driver (R16) was another of the few to fault the play, complaining that, as a piece of writing, it was "old fashioned," that much of its success was "due to our sentimentality over the 'Negro question.'" While he found the play to be a moving theatrical experience, the emotions it engendered were "not relevant" to social and political realities.

Of the anniversary revival of *A Raisin in the Sun* in 1986, a production also shown on PBS's American Playhouse in 1989, Anderson (R44) found Esther Rolle, in the 1989 version, magnificent as Mama and noted particularly the character of Beneatha, who is trying to "find herself" between "the slavish imitation of whites and total reversion to her African roots." Barnes (R40) was another critic to recognize the revival's emphasis on black feminism and nationalism, "these issues of black awareness and black pride," forming a "counterpoint for the entire action." The play was not "simply concerned with the integration of housing." And Collins (R47) said the new production still had a "highly charged currency and relevance," striking with the same "deep fury as Arthur Miller's *Death of a Salesman*." Both plays concern themselves with families in crisis and "bellow out into the universe a lament for the human condition." Yet Erstein (R43) found Hansberry's play "dated," citing the satire of it in George Wolfe's play, *The Colored Museum*, as apt in its suggestion that her characters are now "merely stereotypes of a previous generation's consciousness."

The 1961 film version of *A Raisin in the Sun*, while winning a special award at the Cannes Film Festival and being nominated for the best screenplay of the year by the Screen Writers Guild, received somewhat mixed reviews. Robinson (R49) praised it for transferring the play to the screen "with all of its earthy drama and humor intact." Crowther (R53) thought it to be a fine screen drama in which Sidney Poitier as Walter Lee is "lithe and electric," and Claudia McNeil as Mama is "stolid, voluminous and serene." Yet while the critic for *Ebony* (R55) praised the film's realism which, in part, was due to fifteen percent of it being shot on location around Chicago, the writer for *Newsweek* (R60) found that too much of the action took place in the small apartment.   The *Time* review (R54) declared the movie a "writhing, vital mess of tenement realism," "a superior soap opera in blackface."   And Mekas (R56) proclaimed the movie really "stinks," calling it a "Hollywoodish attempt at a 'message' film," which says the "ideal of the Negro is to get into one of those suburban houses advertised in the *Saturday Evening Post*, with lawns, good neighbors, and rosy kitchens."

Raisin, the 1973 musical adaptation of *A Raisin in the Sun*, while winning the Tony Award, also got mixed reviews from the critics.   Barnes (R134) found it strange but good, perhaps even "better than the play" because it kept all of Hansberry's fine dramatic encounters and cutting, honest dialogue, but was shaped "slightly firmer and better."   Watts (R137), too, appreciated the musical as "good, solid entertainment" that followed the playwright's original drama with "fidelity and respect."   And the *Playboy* review (R145) cited the strong, professional production due to the care and concern of Robert Nemiroff, even while questioning his "compulsiveness" in "mining" his late ex-wife's creations.   Yet others agreed with Yvonne (R143), finding the musical version of the play to be a "weak revival supported primarily by Hansberry's established fame."   Indeed, Kalem (R140) found the play's message of a colorblind society in an era where blacks are concerned with goals of separatism "hopelessly dated."   It is a "soap operetta" in which the dances "have the cumulative frenzy of a Holy Roller meeting," but cannot animate the drama's "faded, though once fashionable faith in integration."

THE SIGN IN SIDNEY BRUSTEIN'S WINDOW (1964). P1

The Characters -- SIDNEY BRUSTEIN, a cynical though idealistic Jewish intellectual in his late thirties who lives in Greenwich Village and runs a newspaper; ALTON SCALES, about twenty-seven, a mulatto Marxist and Sidney's friend and helper who is in love with Gloria; IRIS PARODUS BRUSTEIN, in her late twenties, Sidney's attractive wife and an aspiring actress; MAVIS PARODUS BRYSON, Iris' older, conservative, upper-middle

class sister; DAVID RAGIN, a pessimistic, homosexual playwright and neighbor to Sidney; GLORIA PARODUS, Iris'
younger sister and a high-class prostitute; WALLY O'HARA, a
politician; MAX, a middle-aged artist who helps with Sidney's
newspaper; DETECTIVE.

Plot Summary -- Act I, Scene 1: It is the early evening in late spring
in Sidney Brustein's apartment/courtyard, Greenwich Village,
New York. Sidney and Alton are carrying containers of glasses
from Sidney's defunct "coffee house" business to his apartment.
Sidney tells Alton that the writing in the newspaper he has just
acquired should be objective. It should presume "no commitment,
disavow all engagement, mock all great expectations." They have
a drink and continue to discuss the paper, and Sidney says he has
not yet told his wife, Iris, about buying the newspaper. Iris enters
with groceries and, noticing the glasses, says she does not want
them, the "residue" of his failure, in her living room. Sensing an
argument between the two, Alton leaves. Iris tells Sidney of an
up-coming production of *South Pacific* for which there may be a
part for her. He says she hasn't a chance at getting it, hurting her
and regretting it. They bicker about Iris' faith in analysis, Sidney
informing her that it hasn't done her any good. She says it's
helped her speak up to him and mocks his conception of himself
as an intellectual, proclaiming him actually to be quite narrow-
minded and provincial. She talks about their disappointing sex
life, and he continues to ridicule her faith in analysis. She mentions his existential *angst*, which he denies, and she cites his ulcer
as evidence of it. Sidney makes some literary allusions which
cause Iris, who does not recognize them, to feel inferior, and she
resents this. They then move on to argue about the failure of Sidney's "folk-singing" establishment. She questions what he's going to tell auditors who find no glasses in the place, and they
stumble onto the subject of the newspaper Sidney, to her despair,
has bought. She wants to know how he plans to pay for it, and he
tells her not to worry, he'll get the money when he needs to. Alton and Wally O'Hara enter, Wally carrying placards for his
(Wally's) candidacy. Knowing what they want, Sidney says he's
going to keep his paper out of politics and causes, that it will not
endorse Wally or any other politician. Alton, to goad Sidney, ac-

cuses him of "ostrich-ism" for his refusal to get involved with social and political issues. Sidney says he no longer has the will or
energy to save the world and takes down Wally's poster which
Alton had pinned up. He says cynically he doesn't even care
anymore about improving his own neighborhood. He tells Wally
to "*do things*" if it makes him happy, but not to bother him about
it. Mavis, Iris' older sister, telephones, and Iris speaks with her
as Alton admits he's been seeing her younger sister, Gloria, whom
Iris says, while holding her hand over the telephone receiver, is a
high-fashion model. She hangs up, and Sidney impishly pulls the
pins out of his wife's hair letting it fall down. This habit of his
irritates her. Alton says Sidney would like to see her in a ging-
ham dress with her hair flying. When Wally again suggests that
he "get involved," Sidney says he'd like to escape to the mountains. Sidney says he's arranged for Alton to meet a representative of the Trade and Commerce Commission to assure they will
continue to advertise in the paper. Sidney then approaches Wally,
saying they need someone who is "smooth" and knows how things
are done to get support for the paper. Alton tells Sidney that he
admires the wrong parts of Thoreau, and reads a passage Sidney
has marked on mountains and isolation. Wally calls for a passage
on social consciousness. Alton mocks Sidney's refusal to get involved. Wally and Alton begin to leave, Wally remarking that
he's counting on Sidney.

Act II, Scene 2: Dusk the following week. Max and Alton
are in the apartment quarreling over Max's artwork, which Alton
finds formless and chaotic. Sidney and Alton hang a campaign
sign for Wally in the window which says, "Clean Up Community
Politics and Whip Out Bossism--Vote Reform." They talk over
the content of the next edition of the newspaper. When Alton
criticizes his design for the paper's masthead, the offended Max
starts to leave. Sidney catches him and praises his creative,
avant-garde concepts. Iris enters and invites Alton and Max to
dinner; Max leaves to meet a girl, touting his freedom to Alton.
Reading a letter from her sister, Iris remarks that Gloria has said
that Alton asked her to marry her, and he concurs. Iris and Alton
bicker about his commitment to causes and his racial identity,
which he says is a Negro. Irritated, Alton goes to get some wine
for the dinner, and Iris tells Sidney to keep his mouth shut about

Gloria. He shows her Max's masthead, and she says it looks self-consciously "arty." Sidney resents her expression, and they exchange insults. She exits and cries in the bathroom with Sidney trying to smooth things over. He encourages her to try out for the *South Pacific* part, but she says she wouldn't have a chance to get it because she won't sleep with someone for it. He tries to build up her self esteem as she belittles her own talent. They become quiet, and she tells him how hard it is to audition for a part, and that she won't do it again. Sidney asks her to take down her hair, pulling out the pins and letting it fall. He puts on some bluegrass music and asks her to dance for him. She refuses as her older sister, Mavis, arrives with a dress for her which she does not want. Mavis insistently slips the dress on her sister. She also criticizes the propriety of the sign in the window. Sidney offers her a drink, and she remarks that he's drinking a lot lately. She inquires about Gloria and begins to worry. Iris calls Mavis an anti-Semite, which she denies. Iris defends Gloria's being a high-priced, financially successful whore over Mavis' moral protests. Sidney tells his wife to shut up as she continues to mock the puritanical, anti-sex attitudes of Mavis and middle-class society. Sidney says Gloria's patrons are not concerned with her freedom from Victorian morals but view her as an object for them to use. Mavis says Gloria is sick, and Sidney brings up the subject of Alton's proposal. He teases Mavis about Alton being a communist and says Gloria has not told him her real occupation. He then tells her that Alton is a Negro. Mavis gasps and is appalled at the thought of her prostitute sister marrying a black. David Ragin, a homosexual neighbor and struggling playwright, enters the apartment and asks to borrow some paper. Mavis speculates that he might be a match for Gloria, and Sidney informs her that David's gay. Upon learning of Sidney's newspaper venture, Mavis tells him he needs to grow up and take a real job. The idealistic Sidney says he will not be so "circumscribed." She tells Iris that ignoring her sister's situation is avoiding responsibility, and Sidney agrees. David look at the sign in the window and shakes his head at Sidney's commitment to challenge the political machine. Sidney mocks David's cynicism concerning committing a social act, and makes fun of the dark, existential vision that says all such gestures are meaningless. Sidney asks David what his play means, and he answers that it has to speak for itself. Sidney mocks this affected attitude towards art. Alton returns, and Iris asks David to stay to eat. Iris introduces Mavis to Alton who admires him as a prospect for her sister. Sidney tells her he's the one who has proposed to Gloria. As they eat, Sidney wittily makes fun of the "middle-class" Mavis. She leaves asking pointedly, since they have gotten rid of God, if artists and intellectuals can't provide understanding, who can. Alton and David have words, and Alton leaves saying "hanging out with queers" gets on his nerves. David suggests that Alton has a problem with him because he, himself, is sexually confused. Sidney dismisses this pat gay response to rejection. Iris says, "who cares." Sidney proclaims he does and castigates David for writing plays which say he doesn't care when he really wants to write one that says he's ravaged by a society that won't accept his sexuality. Sidney implores him to act against the injustice done him and not just to act nobly tortured by society's treatment of him. David leaves, rejecting what he calls Sidney's sociological oversimplifications. Iris and Sidney bicker. Soberingly, she tells him she's losing the need to make up with him when they fight. As he leaves, she cries after him that he should "put up a fight for it."

Act II, Scene 1: Just before daybreak the following day, Sidney is beginning to pick his banjo, his plucking turning into *dream* music to which his *dream* Iris, barefooted with flowing hair, mounts the steps to the landing where he is and dances in the shadows. She gives him a final kiss and flees as the real Iris switches on the light. She tells him to come down, but he wants to preserve the ideal moment. He asks her to come up and look at the imaginary mountain pines. She does and gently laughs at his fantasy. She says she can't live in the mountains, that she's turned into an urban wastelander. Recalling when she met him, she tells Sidney she only wears her hair long for him, but actually hates it that way. She says she doesn't like their fantasy woods and wants the city. She says she's changed; she wants to make something of herself. Sidney's intellect is no longer enough to sustain her relationship with him. He says he likes going on the landing and "to the woods" because, there, he feels his place in the primal sense of things. He says he loves her; she asks him to take her back to the city. As the closeness of the moment begins to fade and they descend the stairs, she hears a truck and reminds him that it is the day he has to move the car.

Act II, Scene 2: The scene opens in late summer to the campaign song of Wally O'Hara. Wally is telling Sidney he's going to win. Sidney faces the audience and notes the "disease" that makes a candidate think he has a chance to win. As Sidney fishes for his keys to enter his apartment, David arrives with the news that his play was a hit. He invites David in for a congratulatory drink and asks him to help with the campaign mailings. David questions the idea of human purpose. Sidney, in between answering phone inquiries for the campaign, says that he is committed to human progress again. David leaves, and Sidney notices that Iris, on her way to a cocktail party, is wearing the dress her sister gave her. He notes that his newspaper has lost advertising since it came out supporting Wally's candidacy. She tells him she does not expect him to go to the party with her, that she actually wants to go alone, and that a man there can help her with her career. Sidney's irritation grows as she taunts him with her desire to be independent and do something else with her life other than engaging in conversations about Camus, and the like. She tells him she has gotten a job doing a commercial. When he ridicules this, she says she's being honest with herself, that she's not ever going to be a great actress, and that she just wants something to happen in her life. She leaves, anguishing over his use of the word "happy." Sidney calls to David to come down, and David sheepishly admits that he feels pretty good and is enjoying his sudden celebrity in spite of his insistently absurdist philosophy of life. Sidney tries to get David to find a place for Iris in his next play. David tells him to solve his own marriage problems, and that he won't accept a positive newspaper review of the play from Sidney if he writes a part for Iris in the drama. Wally arrives full of optimism about his election. As David leaves, he responds negatively, and Wally mocks what he calls David's imitation of pessimistic, French intellectuals. He also ridicules David's homosexuality. Wally notes that Iris has been seen with another man, one who can assist her in her career, and gets Sidney his ulcer medicine. Recalling the chivalry of the past, Sidney speculates how one is to conquer the ever-more-complex evils of modern times.

Act II, Scene 3: It is election eve in the fall, and jubilant Sidney's idealism is revived because of Wally's election. He speaks to Alton optimistically about the human race's potential and future. Alton suddenly asks if it's true that Gloria is a prostitute. When Sidney confirms this, Alton berates Gloria as one who treats people as commodities, just as his father, a black porter on a train was used by the white world. He says he won't marry her, and refusing to see Gloria, leaves handing Sidney a note for her. Mavis enters with praise for Sidney and his winning candidate. She gives Sidney a check from her husband for the paper. Mavis talks frankly to Sidney of her limitations and how she's enjoyed, and even understood, some of the conversations she's heard in his apartment. She poignantly recalls her father's poetic spirit and how, mistakenly, she thought her materialistic husband was the same kind of man when she married him. She recalls learning of Greek tragedy from her father, and how he changed their name to Parodus, meaning the "chorus" in a Greek play. She reveals that her marriage is dull, that her husband has a "girl." She's considered divorce, but has resignedly decided to keep what she has, to compromise for the sake of her family and her security. Mavis is happy to hear that Alton will not be marrying Gloria, saying the world is not ready for a mixture of the races. She compliments him on the election again, saying that "Jews have get-up." Tolerating her thoughtless bigotry and appreciating her pain, he kisses her as she leaves. Iris enters with congratulations, mentioning that Gloria is to arrive shortly. She is dressed up and has a new, short hair style. When he asks, she tells him she hasn't told Mavis about the break-up of their marriage. She tells him her new job is doing television commercials for home permanents. While her hair was professionally permed, she lies on the commercial that it is the result of her product. Sidney gets her to admit the hypocrisy of it all. She cries and says she does not want to "play Appalachian anymore," that she's not a child, but that he is. Her father and Sidney are wrong; this world is dirty. He gestures toward the sign in his window and regrets her cynicism. She then reveals that Wally is owned by the corrupt party machine Sidney thought he was opposing. She leaves, telling him that she'll send for her things, and that he should take down his sign.

Act III, Scene 1: Several hours later Gloria arrives and helps
the drunk Sidney up to the sofa. She recognizes that he's having
an ulcer attack and gets him some milk, which he spits out. He is
wallowing in self pity and lamenting the loss of his idealism. He
says Iris is gone. David enters and Sidney now compliments his
pessimistic, existential outlook on life. Sidney runs to the bathroom and Gloria and David banter, she telling him to stop probing
into her life and to leave. As he does, Sidney returns. She tells
him she was hurt by a man she was with, that there's violence in
her profession. She agrees to have a drink with him, saying she's
going to marry Alton. Sidney, knowing the disappointment that
will come to her, tells Gloria that Alton really loves her and hands
her the letter he left for her. As she takes some drugs with her
drink, she bewails life, cynically mocking Alton for his color and
his male ways. To calm her down, Sidney puts on a record and
they dance. Sidney philosophizes about the meaninglessness of
things as David enters and concurs, and they all dance, chanting
about the absurdity of life. As Sidney dozes on the sofa, David
and Gloria continue to dance and talk about their disappoint-
ments. He asks Gloria up to his apartment to help and console a
young man he brought home with him. He leaves, but instead of
going up to his flat, in a moment of self-certainty, Gloria takes
her bottle of pills and goes into the bathroom.

Act III, Scene 2: Early the next morning, a detective is
questioning Iris about Gloria, who died that night of an overdose
in the bathroom. Wally stops by, and, with Sidney's rejection of
him, tells Sidney that to survive in this world you must
"negotiate" and know where the power is. He says he's going to
help people, but the narcotics problem is a complicated one that
he can't so easily condemn any more. He lets Sidney know that
his paper should not deal with such issues again if he wants to
keep it going. Sidney berates Wally, saying that Gloria died trying to accept a vision of reality such as Wally's. He tells Wally
he's more cynical now, and will fight even harder against what
Wally stands for--collusion with the tools of power. Wally calls
him a fool for his innocence and idealism, while Sidney proclaims
he believes energy can move and change things for the better.
Wally leaves, glancing at the sign in Sidney's window, and Iris
weeps for her sister and her marriage. Sidney says that tomorrow

they will make something strong of their sorrow.

Productions and Credits -- Broadway: Longacre Theatre, New
York City, October 15, 1964. (Moved December 29, 1964 to
Henry Miller's Theatre, New York City.) 101 performances.
 Producers: Burt C. D'Lugoff, Robert Nemiroff, J.I. Jahre
 Director: Peter Kass
 Scenery: Jack Blackman
 Costumes: Fred Voelpel
 Lighting: Jules Fisher
 Campaign Song: Ernie Sheldon (recorded by the Moon-
  shiners)
 Cast: Sidney Brustein -- Gabriel Dell
   Iris Parodus Brustein -- Rita Moreno
   Alton Scales -- Ben Aliza
   Wally O'Hara -- Frank Schofield
   Max -- Dolph Sweet
   Mavis Parodus Bryson -- Alice Ghostley
   David Ragin -- John Alderman
   Gloria Parodus -- Cynthia O'Neal (succeeded by
    Louise Sorel)
   Policeman -- Josip Elic

Revival with Music: Broadway: Longacre Theatre, New York
City, January 26, 1972. 5 performances. Adapted by Robert
Nemiroff and Charlotte Zaltzberg.
 Producer: Robert Nemiroff
 Director: Alan Schneider
 Music: Gary William Friedman
 Lyrics: Ray Errol Fox
 Setting: William Ritman
 Costumes: Thenol V. Aldredge
 Lighting: Richard Nelson
 Musical Director: Mark Schlefer
 Musical Arranger: Gary William Friedman
 Musical Staging: Rhoda Levine
 Cast: Sidney Brustein -- Hal Linden
   Iris Parodus Brustein -- Zohra Lampert
   Alton Scales -- John Danelle

Wally O'Hara -- Mason Adams
Max -- Dolph Sweet
Mavis Parodus Bryson -- Frances Sternhagen
David Ragin -- William Atherton
Gloria Parodus -- Kelly Wood
Singers -- Danny Beard, Pendleton Brown, John Lan-
    sing, Arnetia Walker

Reviews (play and play with music) -- R63-R91.

Other Secondary Sources -- S9, S14, S15, S16, S17, S19, S20,
    S21, S27, S29, S42, S60, S63, S69, S79, S81, S84, S87, S92,
    S96, S105, S114, S128, S130, S140, S144.

Critical Overview -- After *A Raisin in the Sun*, *The Sign in Sidney
    Brustein's Window* became Hansberry's second produced play,
    opening October 15, 1964 at the Longacre Theatre. Critics, who
    had perhaps expected another play about the African-American
    experience, were surprised by one with a Jew as protagonist, set
    in Bohemian Greenwich Village, and populated by mostly white
    characters who struggle with problems pertaining to the conflict
    of their idealism with the complex realities of actual life. It was a
    play of ideas which was critical of cynical attitudes toward life,
    and one that called upon intellectuals and artists to involve them-
    selves in social issues and to make a difference, even when their
    activities seemed futile (S140).
        Scholarly appraisals of *The Sign in Sidney Brustein's Win-
    dow*, while fewer than those concerning *A Raisin in the Sun*, fo-
    cus on Hansberry's feeling that her own generation had fallen un-
    der the pessimistic aura of postwar existentialism with its insis-
    tence on the absurdity of human experience. Her play, she said,
    was one that was trying to "examine something of the nature of
    commitment. It happens to be...one of the leading problems be-
    fore my generation here: what to identify with, what to become
    involved in; what to take a stand on; what even to believe in at
    all" (S79). The play, she said, was to be an antidote to "the
    vogue of unmodified despair" in the works of such playwrights as
    Beckett, Genet, and Albee (S79, S140). Holton (S29), therefore,
    views the play as one dealing with how the intellectual must come

to see the world with "open-eyed commitment," its themes relating to the "plight of the intellectual in a corrupt society," in which he must nonetheless live "and from which he cannot flee." Bigsby (S130), likewise, sees the play as one which dramatizes the idea of "commitment in all its guises--political, racial, sexual--and an awareness of betrayal as a central motif in human existence."

Sidney Brustein, and the fact that he is Jewish, is of importance to Schiff, who asserts that a "sensitive concept of the Jewish experience as archetypal" is a subtext of *The Sign in Sidney Brustein's Window*. He is "the Jew who has found his niche in society and occupies it with the same aplomb with which he wears his identity," and because he has known prejudice and rejection, he relates to all, regardless of race, sex, or social status. Schiff (S84) concludes that Sidney emerges as not just the Jew "making his way in a frequently hostile society and helping others as he moves along, but as unaccommodated man, determined to shape his world to more human proportions." Carter (S128) agrees, noting that Sidney's Jewishness, "in spite of the many weaknesses he displays, enables Hansberry to express through him her admiration for the Jews' historical resilience in oppression and adversity and for the sensitivity, courage, and insight that many derived from this." He is, Carter (S128) asserts, the "chief connection" of the various cultural interests, ethnic and social identities, political and aesthetic attitudes, and philosophies personified by the other characters (S128).

Yet Sidney is portrayed as a real man in the real world. Of his harsh, seemingly insensitive words to David, the homosexual playwright, Carter (S114) suggests that they demonstrate "how hard it is for someone of even Sidney's broadmindedness and experience to eradicate all the traces of prejudices (ethnic or other) that are so thoroughly ingrained in his culture"; that it "is possible for a person to act or think in a way that is simultaneously right and wrong," and that "it is therefore excruciatingly difficult to choose the proper course for the appropriate reasons."

Cheney (S87) identifies sexuality in the play as one of Hansberry's major concerns, suggesting that the playwright seems to be saying (most notably through the relationship of Sidney and Iris, the sexual problems of Iris' sisters, Alton's treatment of Gloria, as well as the fact of David's homosexuality) "that not until one's sexual behavior is mature, devoid of fantasy and there-fore honest, will growth or personal satisfaction be possible." Hansberry "pleads for maturity and commitment in sexuality and creativity--whatever form each may take."

Perhaps because *The Sign in Sidney Brustein's Window* was not a "black play" that dealt specifically with issues of African-American liberation, as well as the fact that Hansberry had writ-ten a play dealing with a myriad of complex ideas, many review-ers were confused by it and reacted negatively. In fact, the play, which under normal circumstances would have closed rather quickly due to the weak notices it received, continued to run for a total of 101 performances due only to the dedication, sacrifices, donations, and support of people connected to the theater who made keeping a serious, mature, drama open on Broadway a *cause*. It finally closed the night of Hansberry's death (S79, S140).

Typical criticism involved what was felt to be a lack of focus in the play, a feeling that Hansberry was trying to deal with too many issues. Chapman (R63), for instance, said that, unlike *A Raisin in the Sun, The Sign in Sidney Brustein's Window* was "not warm, compact, and direct," that it was "wordy and played scene by scene, not as a theatrical whole." McClain (R65) had a similar impression, saying that while a great deal of the dialogue was good, it took "too long to get it sorted out." And Taubman (R67), while admitting that there were lines in the play that "shine with humor, tremble with feeling and summon up a vision of wis-dom and integrity," found it lacking in concision and cohesion. It seemed that it was merely a vehicle for Hansberry to "tick off some of her pet peeves," which included making a "mordant comment on homosexuality." Kerr (R64) concluded that there were good things in a play packaged too loosely. And Clurman (R76) complained that, while the play aimed at depicting the "morass of our times," the disillusionment of the urban life among the "intelligentsia," and then sought to suggest a "cure" through "commonsense, kindness, and understanding," nothing was dramatized. Self-explanation, he said, "takes the place of revela-tion." Most pointedly, Gilman (R72) accused Hansberry of creat-ing an "inverted miracle" in which she "manages to distort so many things--taste, intelligence, craft--and be simultaneously perverse as a dramatist, social commentator, political oracle, and moral visionary." The drama is a "union of bitchiness with sentimentality."

Answering the play's detractors, Neal (R79) claimed that they had "missed the point." *The Sign in Sidney Brustein's Window* is concerned with the same thing as *A Raisin in the Sun*: "the necessity of making ethical decisions of a fundamental nature" that will define the relationships of all people, black and white. Lewis (R80) said it was a play that just missed being great and proved that Hansberry, who wrote a "delectable chiaroscuro of life in the Village," was not just a "one-shot" author. Redding agreed, praising the play for dealing with "modern man in confrontation with a world he never made and which he must remake to conform to the definition of himself" (R82).

Of a short-lived 1972 revival of the play, which included musical interludes, Barnes (R84) complained that the drama was "flawed" and at times sunk into melodrama, yet had "the good red-blood of Broadway success running through it." Heldman (R88) thought the play, in spite of its weaknesses, "a wise, tender, tasteful portrait of humanity that is also very funny," but found the musical quartet acting like a Greek chorus "entirely superfluous." Gottfried (R85) wrote that the original production had been "clumsy" and the musical revival was, too. Yet while Watts (R87) found the original production "too cluttered for its own good," he insisted the musical revival had a "number of admirable scenes and several striking and original characters."

TO BE YOUNG, GIFTED AND BLACK (1969). P9

The Characters -- TWO YOUNG BLACK ACTRESSES, ideally one of whom should have appealing youthful qualities of Hansberry as a school girl and college coed, while the other should exhibit the greater maturity of vision and intellectual depth of the playwright in her early thirties. The first of these actresses, in addition to playing Ruth in the Prologue, plays the 1st Actress (1:1, 4 and 7; 2:5), Candace, Beneatha, the Coed, Zen Disciple, 2nd Actress (2:6), and 3rd Actress (Epilogue). The second actress plays the playwright (Prologue, 1:6 and 9; 2:6 and Epilogue), 1st Actress (1:2), Sarah (1:3), 4th Girl (1:4), Ruth (1:6 and 9), Domestic (1:7), 3rd Actress (2:1 and 3), and "She" (2:5); AN OLDER BLACK ACTRESS, who plays Mama, the various Mothers; TWO WHITE ACTRESSES, one of whom should be young and attractive and play Gloria Mariela, Autograph Hound, and Iris. The other, somewhat older, plays Mavis, Pale Hecate, and Juno; A BLACK ACTOR who plays Walter, Father, Leader, Hannibal, 2nd Boy, Monasse, Black Student, Tshembe, and Waiter; A WHITE ACTOR who plays Sidney, The Man, Zeb, Professor, Linder, Southerner, Hermit, and "He."

Plot Summary -- Act I, Prologue: A recorded voice says "My name is Lorraine Hansberry. I am a writer." The voice of the Hansberry character goes on to express her artistic credo, her wish to celebrate and create illumination and communion between people. A switch to a scene from *A Raisin in the Sun* (Act I, Scene 1) in which Walter expresses his dismay of how "colored women" don't support their men's dreams. A switch back to the recorded voice of the Hansberry character which says that she believes that every human being is dramatically interesting. A switch to *The Sign in Sidney Brustein's Window* and a morose Sidney Brustein asking himself who and why he is, the existential questions that spring from the fact of mortality. A switch to Mavis telling Sidney about the realities of her disappointing life and her husband's girlfriend (Act II, Scene 2). A switch to Gloria telling Sidney about a picture of Goya in which a woman, for good luck, is reaching to grab the teeth of a man who has just been hanged. She says the painting reflects her life (Act II, Scene 1). A switch to Mama of *A Raisin in the Sun* saying that the time to love somebody the most is when he's at his lowest, not when things are fine and it's easy (Act III). A switch to the Playwright addressing a black writers' conference who speaks of her life on the Southside of Chicago out of which her plays have grown.

Act I, Sequence 1: The 1st Actress says that all travelers in Chicago should ride the elevated train and see the lives of the black people on their back porches. The 2nd Actress remarks on the shabby living conditions of the people, but also of how clean and scrubbed they look. A Woman says that her people are poor; a Mother and Father say they are tired. The Man, a white official representing the State of Illinois, enters reading the birth registration record of Lorraine Hansberry to her Father and Mother for confirmation. Father and Mother say they should be listed racially not as Negro but as Black.

Act I, Sequence 2: 1st Actress reminisces about her life in the summers on the Southside, the streets full of games and rhymes, which The Children join in singing. These voices permeate her commentary on the bygone times. The 2nd Actress recollects the steamy summer evenings on the back porches with the smell of lemons and melons in the air. The Mother tells Father, Daughter, Girl, and 2nd Actress past experiences in Tennessee and the beautiful Kentucky hills and how her mother's father had run away from his master when he was a little boy. She remembers visiting her grandmother and being surprised at how old and wrinkled she was, and how she had died the following summer.

Act I, Sequence 3: A switch to a scene from *The Drinking Gourd* in which Sarah and Hannibal greet lovingly. She warns him he'll get in trouble for stealing their master's Bible, and he surprises her with the news that he can actually read it. She warns him what can happen if the whites find out he can read. But he tells her not to worry, that they aren't going to find out. He gazes at and wonders about the stars, calling the big dipper "The ol' Drinking Gourd" which will point them to the north and freedom. Sarah cautions Hannibal to bend a little, but he says he's the only kind of slave he can be: a bad one who won't bend. He happily grinds down his master everyday he can get away with pretending to be stupid instead of smart, lazy instead of quick. Hannibal remarks that every slave should run off before he dies, and Sarah expresses fear at the prospect of doing so. He runs off, telling her that he'll come back and buy her. A switch to Zeb Dudley telling a preacher that he's not going to be a poor white and plans to own some slaves of his own in a year.

Act I, Sequence 4: The 1st Actress talks about not coming from a poverty-stricken home, that her father ran for Congress as a Republican and believed in private enterprise and made, in terms of their community, a fortune. She recalls being thought of as a "rich" girl and how the children in her kindergarten class beat her up when she wore a white fur to school. It was then that she became a rebel. The 2nd Actress recalls getting the white fur as a gift for Christmas and hating it over the "oohs and aahs" of her relatives. The 1st Actress says the "oohs and aahs" prevailed, however, and she was sent to school in it. But she wanted to court the friendship of the tough ghetto children. The Girls accuse the 1st Actress of offensive remarks and hit her. This experience etches terror and violence in her mind. A switch to Englewood High School and the 1st Actress recalling her admiration for Shakespeare under the instruction of a demanding teacher they cruelly called Pale Hecate. Pale Hecate instructs her English class with rigor and love of the English language. A switch as the 1st Actress remembers white students attacking them with baseball bats and how they fought back.

Act I, Sequence 5: The Professor speaks of Candace, who is more interested in the cold, clean, snow-covered Wisconsin hills than in her college course in fine arts. He wonders who her slave ancestors were and speculates that many types of racial blood flow in her veins. A switch as Mother talks to Candace of how she (Candace) was fascinated with Africa when she was a child. A switch back to the Professor who watches Candace in the snow. She remarks to Monasse, an African, that he need not stay outside if it is too cold, but he likes the beauty of the scene. Monasse asks her to have tea with him, and she expresses dismay that he is not passionate about revolution in Africa. A switch to her dorm where she expresses her affection for Monasse to Mariela. Mariela tells her she's pregnant. Candace suggests an abortion, but Mariela says she wants the baby, and that's why she didn't "use" anything to prevent it. She thinks her boyfriend will marry her, and she will quit college, having found what she wanted. A switch to Candace defending Mariela against Monasse's condemnation of her morals. Expressing his cultural sexism, he excuses Mariela's boyfriend. Candace defends the use of contraceptives. He says it would be against his principles to sleep with her under the circumstances characterizing their present relationship. The Professor says Candace was moved to try to change Monasse's mind in behalf of American women and world emancipation.

Act I, Sequence 6: A Catholic funeral mass is taking place, and Juno Boyle says that these things have nothing to do with the will of God. Where was the Blessed Virgin when her son was

riddled with bullets, she painfully asks. The Playwright enters
and, as Juno expresses her heartache and resentment, remembers
how she wandered into the university theater and saw the Irish
agony in *Juno and the Paycock.* She believes that's when the
idea of writing entered her consciousness. A switch to *A Raisin
in the Sun* (Act II, Scene 1) in which Beneatha and Walter Lee
dance to African music and celebrate, momentarily, their primal
race consciousness.

Act I, Sequence 7: The 1st Actress is at a Baptist funeral in
Harlem where she observes and thinks about the strong, young
man in the casket who was shot and killed by the "cops." A
switch to New York where the 2nd Actress is writing her friend
back home of her experience there. She relates that she now
works for Paul Robeson's *Freedom*, a black paper, and that she's
slimmer than she was. She sees only foreign movies, eats foreign
foods, and is sick of poverty, lynching, stupid wars, and "the universal mistreatment of my people." She concludes that she's supposed to get married in September. A switch to a Domestic who
relates her resentment of the taunts of white boys who look at her
as a sexual object, and her trembling rage at having to work in the
house of a white woman. A switch to the 2nd Actress who recalls
a poor black woman at Coney Island, a mother determined to
have a good time with her child.

Act I, Sequence 8: The Playwright is writing a letter saying
that she loves the person who will receive it, and that she's finally
decided that she will become a writer. A switch, and the cast
sings a child's rhyming song as the Actor and Actress say lines
from some of the previous scenes of the play. The Playwright,
addressing her husband, says she is at her typewriter feeling cold,
disillusioned, angry, and tired. The Playwright recalls voices
from her past as the Actress, Actor, and other characters continue
to repeat lines heard earlier and say things that create a stream of
consciousness sense of Africa, creativity, violence, imagination,
love, etc. A switch to a letter the Playwright is composing for her
mother. It speaks of the soon-to-open *A Raisin in the Sun*, a play
she says tells the truth about Negroes and their lives.

Act I, Sequence 9: The scene from *A Raisin in the Sun* (Act
III) in which Walter tells his family that he's contacted Linder so
that they might sell their house in the white neighborhood back to

him at a profit. The episode ends with Walter, finally, refusing to deal with the whites. The Playwright relates how she wants to relate the sad passion of her people in the way Sean O'Casey conveys the wail of the Irish poor in his plays.

Act II, Sequence 1: A Coed, a Southerner, an Autograph Hound, and a Black Student write to Hansberry, all expressing admiration for her. She is a playwright and a celebrity. A switch to the 1st Actress, who answers a letter from a southern white student about the "Negro Question" and Martin Luther King. She responds that blacks need to be revolutionary in any way necessary to achieve justice. The 2nd Actress responds graciously to a letter from a Chinese professor, Mme. Chen. And the 3rd Actress tells Mme. Chen that she is finally at work on another play, *The Sign in Sidney Brustein's Window*.

Act II, Sequence 2: A scene from *The Sign in Sidney Brustein's Window* (Act I, Scene 1) in which Iris and Sidney bicker about her career goals, psychoanalysis, his intellectual pretense, and the general unhappiness of their marriage.

Act II, Sequence 3: The 3rd Actress writes Mme. Chen of her play, *Les Blancs*, which is set in modern Africa, and another, *Toussaint*, which takes place in the years of the Haitian Revolution. She also mentions a musical based on Oliver La Farge's novel of Indian life, *Laughing Boy*. The 2nd Actress then gives a summary of a play about war and peace in which an old hermit comes upon a group of children in a forest after a nuclear war. He wants to impart his knowledge of civilization about them. A switch to the Hermit talking to the children. He asks them to consider the idea of beauty. He sings "Greensleeves" to them and identifies what they hear as a "melody," part of a great body of pleasure called "music." He gets the children to sing. A switch to the 2nd Actress writing Mme. Chen, saying in five years they'll know whether she (2nd Actress) is merely a dreamer. A switch back to the Hermit answering a child's question as to what "use" music is. He finds this a difficult question to address on a rational level. A switch to the 3rd Actress who writes in a letter of Hemingway's suicide and her frustration with the slow creative process and how she desperately desires to complete a manuscript that makes some kind of contribution. A switch to Tshembe who says that he does not hate whites, and that the whites, who hate the blacks and have raided Africa for three centuries, never "loved" the white race, either (*Les Blancs*, Act I, Scene 3). A switch, and the 3rd Actress is saying how she'd love to be at a party tonight, but that she is very alone and having trouble with her work. The 3rd and 2nd Actresses converse, and a satire of contemporary notions of drama, in which it is up to the audience to determine what the playwright's "universal" abstractions mean, results. The play, counsels the 2nd Actress, must speak for itself. She, speaking from the point of view of modern existential philosophy, ruminates on the modern theme of "guilt." We are all guilty and, therefore, released of the obligation for meaningful social action. A switch to Sidney Brustein who laments that he has lost the will of his ancestors to smite evil; now one just "holds one's guts and takes a pill." The 2nd and 3rd Actresses continue to talk of the life of a writer. The 3rd Actress says she goes on with it because she cares. And she finally reaches a point of exhilaration when she is able to write again.

Act II, Sequence 4: *The Sign in Sidney Brustein's Window* (Act II, Scene 2) in which Mavis worries about her sister Gloria because she is a prostitute and, concurrently, over the fact that she may marry a Negro. Her provincialism and bigotry are satirized. However, her closing thought--if one can't get compassion and understanding from artists and other people of intelligence and creativity, wherever can one find it--calls her intellectually-sophisticated and cynical detractors, like Sidney, into question.

Act II, Sequence 5: The 1st Actress is reciting a statement about black drama and black arts which echoes a prospectus for a Harlem community theater. A switch, and She (a black intellectual) and He, a white friend, discuss the Presidential inauguration where Marian Anderson sang and the black butler was dressed in tails. She notes the irony that "The brother was opening doors and the sister was singin'!" He chastises her for using affected, low-class black speech, as do so many other black intellectuals. She defends it, saying it adds vitality, strength, and poetry to language when black idiom is used. He says the practice is a result of middle-class blacks' guilt of having moved above lower-class Negroes. Yet they still guiltily feel the need to reach back down to them. When she vehemently objects to his insinuations, he also accuses her of being a "racial megalomaniac." She accuses him of bringing up race all the time, that it was he who wrote how Negroes were going to be subsumed into the values of white suburbia and lose their souls. He says that's sadly true, and that Negroes are "different." She tells him not to worry about her people losing their souls, that they have their feet firmly on the materialistic ground of the ghetto and are too close to its horrors to romance about it. Their triumphant spirit will "spill out and over the world" through their art "like mighty waves of a great spiritual." She tells the audience she could no longer hear him as she envisioned all the great black artists bringing the earth a heavenly brightness. Moved to a gesture of unity, he begins to sing the spiritual along with her and the guests. A switch to the 1st Actress who expresses a theory of black theater which will be, unlike the tradition of Brecht, a realistic theater primarily of emotion, with a goal to move people. A switch to *The Sign in Sidney Brustein's Window* (Act II, Scene 3) in which Alton recollects his black father's sacrificed life working as a porter on the train and his mother, over the deep resentment of his father, having to bring left-over food home from the kitchen of her white employer so that the family could survive. His father's lament at not wanting "white man's leavings," is his, too, Alton tells Sidney.

Act II, Sequence 6: The 1st and 2nd Actresses state their perspectives on life, art, and commitment. The 2nd Actress mentions that she is sick, but, when her health is back, will go South to see the beautiful, young, determined blacks who face the "hose fire" in Birmingham. A switch to the Playwright who is presenting awards for a young black writers conference. She addresses them respectfully as being young, gifted and black, telling them that they know, having experienced despair or racial injustice, what the resiliency and spirit of life are. She tells them the nation needs their gifts!

Act II, Epilogue: The 1st Actress says that she's to fly to a clinic in Boston. The 1st and 2nd Actors talk about the blue of the sky and all the twilights ever known. The 2nd Actress speaks of the smell of the earth and loving life. The 3rd Actress proclaims, "Long live good life! And beauty--and love!" The 4th Actress, in the voice of a journal entry, says that if anything should happen, that "someone will complete my thoughts." The Playwright says, finally, "This last should be the least difficult--

since there are so many who think as I do."

Productions and Credits -- Off-Broadway: Cherry Lane Theatre, New York City, January 2, 1969. 380 performances. Adapted from the works of Lorraine Hansberry by Robert Nemiroff.

> Producers: Harry Belafonte, Chiz Shultz, Edgar Lansbury, Burt D'Lugoff, Ray Larsen, Robert Nemiroff
> Director: Gene Frankel
> Setting: Merrill Sindler
> Lighting: Barry Arnold
> Musical Coordinator: William Eaton
> Sound: Gigi Cascio
> Photographic Effects: Stuart Bigger
> Production Consultant: Charlotte Zaltzberg
> Cast: Barbara Baxley, John Bean, Rita Gardner, Gertrude Jeannette, Janet League, Stephen Strimpell, Cicely Tyson, Andre Womble

> The actors listed above were succeeded during the season by Stephanie Elliot, Bruce Hall, Dolores Sutton, Alice Borden, William Suplee, Moses Gunn, Bernard Ward, Tina Sattin.

> The actors played the roles of Ruth, Candace, Beneatha, Coed, Zen Disciple, 1st Actress, 2nd Actress, 3rd Actress, "She," Mama, Mothers, Gloria Mariela, Autograph Hound, Iris, Mavis, Pale Hecate, Juno, Walter, Father, Leader, Hannibal, 2nd Boy, Monasse, Black Student, Tshembe, Waiter, Sidney, The Man, Zeb, Professor, Linder, Southerner, Hermit, "He."

Reviews (play) -- R92-R108.

Other Secondary Sources -- S25, S28, S62, S76, S79, S87, S139, S140.

Critical Overview -- As early as 1965, Robert Nemiroff, Hansberry's literary executor, was reviewing and editing her published and unpublished writings. One result was *To Be Young, Gifted and Black*, which opened at New York's Cherry Lane Theatre and became the longest running off-Broadway play produced in

1969 (S79). The drama is a two-act "collage" consisting of elements from Hansberry's published plays, as well as fragments from articles, speeches, letters, and other writings. On a sparse stage, with the help of innovative lighting, music, and sound effects, the audience is ushered from Hansberry's childhood to her death, a few actors playing various roles to create a free-flowing but chronological "portrait of the artist" who was to achieve such great fame in her short life.

There has been little scholarly analysis of the play, perhaps because others agree with Carter (S128), who, in the Forward to his book on Hansberry's drama, states that he chose not to discuss *To Be Young, Gifted and Black* (neither the stage play (P9) nor the book-length "informal autobiography" (P8) of the same title) due to the fact that both, though constructed from Hansberry's own words and works, were nonetheless creations of adaptor Robert Nemiroff. Lester (S25) notes that the drama has rightfully brought attention to her other works and says it reveals that Hansberry was a "black artist who lived beyond anger," and that while perhaps angry, "anger did not define her art." While McKelly (S139) finds that in *To Be Young, Gifted and Black*, Hansberry "contradicted her own role as the author of [*A*] *Raisin* [*in the Sun*]" by presenting "an artist less amenable to the white cultural establishment and, as a result, more threatening to white political authority." The black artist is portrayed as one being "as much inclined to an art of insurrection as to an art of the beautiful," the play pointing out the "fundamental tension between art and politics which is the black artist's responsibility, or curse." And Gresham (S62) analyzes the play's ample evidence of Hansberry's "classical artistry as a prose stylist," as well as her mastery of the essay form.

Theatrical reviews were mainly positive. Silber (R95) thought *To Be Young, Gifted and Black* to be not merely a play of sentimental memories, but "an intensely theatrical and emotionally stirring event." Clurman (R96) agreed, noting that it showed Hansberry's "sweetness and balance, a healthy intelligence, a secure spirit." Hentoff (R97) found the drama a "whirl of probing, celebrating, hoping, laughing, despairing, and moving on." While Barnes (R99) thought the play interesting in that it showed the playwright to be "far more militant in her letters than in her plays," concluding that Hansberry was "clearly, and understandably, more radical as a person than as a playwright." And Shorey (R105) saw *To Be Young, Gifted and Black* as a study in "black definitions and the search for meaning," as well as a chronicle of the playwright's "mild flirtations with revolutionary, even Communist, ideas."

On the other hand, Duberman (R92) concluded that *To Be Young, Gifted and Black* showed some of Hansberry's attitudes to be "decidedly out of fashion with black playwrights now," the self-portrait she draws of herself as a young co-ed resembling a heroine in any standard *McCall's* serial. And Oliver (R94) faulted the play because "excerpts from letters and journals are better read privately than heard." Perhaps the most vehement detractor was Weales (R98), who proclaimed the play a "disgraceful presentation" that "made a mockery of Miss Hansberry's talents, destroyed everything that is good and subtle in her work." "If Nemiroff's mosaic were to be taken at face value," he asserted, "it would be necessary to assume that Miss Hansberry was a gushy little girl."

LES BLANCS (1970). P2

The Characters -- TSHEMBE MATOSEH, a black African living in England who returns to Africa to attend his father's funeral; ABIOSEH MATOSEH, Tshembe's brother, soon to take his final vows as a Catholic priest; ERIC, Tshembe and Abioseh's half-white, alcoholic, homosexual brother; CHARLIE MORRIS, an American journalist; MADAME NEILSEN, a genteel European woman and wife of the founder of the Mission; DR. MARTA GOTTERLING, and DR. WILL DEKOVEN, members of the Mission staff; PETER, a black porter/servant at the Mission; MAJOR GEORGE RICE, a colonial officer; THE WOMAN, an African dancer; NGAGO, a graceful warrior; an AFRICAN CHILD; a PRISONER; SOLDIERS; AFRICAN VILLAGERS and WARRIORS.

Plot Summary -- Act I, Prologue: At twilight amid the sounds of the jungle, a woman, dressed and painted for war, does a war dance, pulling a spear from the earth with great strength and raising it high.

Act I, Scene 1: It is mid-afternoon at the Mission as Peter, patronizingly referring to him as "Bwana," escorts Charlie onto the stage and tells him to sit and cool off. Dr. Marta Gotterling welcomes him to the Mission. She continues treating a young boy and says that Reverend Neilsen couldn't be there because he had to go across the river to perform a wedding, a funeral, and twelve baptisms. She continues to treat patients and informs Charlie that the lack of sanitation around the Mission hospital is a small price to pay to get the village people comfortable enough to come for treatment. As he drinks a scotch, she tells him, to his interest and amazement, that they have to do without refrigeration and other electrical conveniences. Marta remarks that the Reverend Neilsen is like a father to them all, white and black. As he questions her, she says that valuables must be locked up, that the Africans have no sense of private property, and that whites should not romanticize Africa. Dr. DeKoven enters, and after introducing him to Charlie, Marta leaves to examine a patient. Major Rice is heard off-stage and enters, bluntly inquiring as to Charlie's identity. Rice says the shots heard were the result of flushing out some terrorists. Soldiers enter with a bloody prisoner whom, to Rice's irritation, Dr. DeKoven refuses to identify as a former worker at the Mission. Rice tells Charlie that there is, indeed, a terrorist problem. Rice asks to read any dispatches Charlie wants to send, and Charlie refuses. Rice leaves, and DeKoven tells the reporter that the West does not know about the terrorist war there. Marta escorts Madame Neilsen onto the stage as the elderly woman asks who was butchered today. Madame graciously greets Charlie. She remarks about Eric's alcoholism and DeKoven giving liquor to him. She tells Charlie that the drums announce the funeral of an important person and tells of how she was taught the native tongue and customs by a now deceased village woman named Aquah. Charlie is amazed. She goes on to say that there has been a change, that the villagers no longer relate to the Europeans with affection. It started with a change in attitude of Old Abioseh, the husband of Aquah. She says for seven years, many of the natives have refused to come to the Mission. Eric comes into the compound, and Madame asks him to show Charlie to his

room. She points out Eric's light complexion to Charlie and remains on the verandah as the two exit. She will sit and leave the
world to its "deceptions."

Act I, Scene 2: It is dusk and Eric is drinking from a bottle.
His brother, Tshembe, enters and, with mutual African signs of
greeting, they embrace each other. Surprised that Tshembe even
came, Eric tells his disappointed brother that their father died the
night before. Tshembe gives Eric some American cigarettes as
they wonder if their other brother, Abioseh, will come. Eric is
surprised to learn Tshembe has a European wife and child. He
describes his wife to Eric who questions her white beauty. They
talk about the insurgent African leader, Kumalo, who will be returning from Europe, and the absurdity of European political
protocol. Eric wonders if Kumalo will support the terrorists when
he returns. Tshembe tells him not to refer to them as terrorists (a
colonial word) but instead as revolutionaries, rebels, or fools.
Tshembe is dismayed that Eric seems to be unappreciative of their
father and mother's native ways. Abioseh arrives and greets his
brothers. Tshembe speaks of seeing Europe and America,
Abioseh referring to his wandering brother as "Ishmael." Tshembe relates how he finally got to Europe, and Abioseh is alarmed at
the hint that his brother might be sympathetic with the terrorists.
Abioseh says that the way to make Africa African is to work
peacefully with the settlers, and that the fanatical terrorists will
only give the whites an excuse to use violence themselves.
Tshembe changes the subject, saying he is not concerned with
African liberation, that, in the spirit of Camus' philosophy, he
made a decision to direct his own life and discover himself.
Tshembe then says they should participate in their father's funeral
ceremony in the traditional, non-western way, to which Abioseh
seems to object. It is then revealed that he will soon take his final
vows as a Catholic priest. Tshembe mocks his brother for turning
his back on their ancestral customs, and Abioseh counters with
his dream that someday there will be a black African Cardinal.
Tshembe equates the Catholic church to western oppression, and
he tells Abioseh that Jesus would not approve of priests and tem-
ples. He leaves wearing his African ceremonial robes while
Abioseh tells him he is condemning himself to hell.

Act I, Scene 3: In the evening, Madame Neilsen sits on the

verandah. At her suggestion that Charlie and Marta go for a walk
by the river, Marta refuses, saying that it is dangerous and that
terrorism is no joke. References are made to recently murdered
white families, and Marta says that sometimes the black servants
are in on the slaughter. Rice enters with news of another attack
and that another white family has been wiped out. Rice condemns
all the Africans, calling them savages. He leaves with DeKoven
to deal with security, and Tshembe arrives, Madame relishing his
presence. She notes that he now wears his hair like a European.
He tells her he's been to her homeland and presents her with a
cuckoo clock from there. She asks soberly if he's seen Eric.
Rice, DeKoven, and the Major insist that they take security seriously. He is suspicious of Tshembe because he is black and because he does not have his "papers" with him. Rice, ignoring
Madame's disgust, examines Tshembe's arms for markings that
would link him to the terrorists. Tshembe then reveals, shocking
Madame, that he is dressed in African garb because he came to
his father's funeral. Rice stiffly offers his condolences and proclaims the area under martial jurisdiction and that all should arm
themselves. They all resist this extreme suggestion. Rice then
recites to Charlie how Africa is his home, and that it is the Europeans who have made something of the place which they intend to
defend. Rice leaves. Irritated with his speech, Madame says
she's going to bed. She tells Tshembe she's pleased he got to visit
her homeland and see her mountains there. She leaves, and
Tshembe and Charlie have a drink and talk, Charlie disarming the
stiff Tshembe with his American straightforwardness. He mockingly informs Charlie that he has had enough talks with white intellectuals who supposedly hate imperialism and want to dig out
his frustrations to find his primal, African soul. Tshembe says,
while in America he found American apartheid and racism enrag-
ing. He informs Charlie that he is an African with 300 years of
oppression in back of him, not an American Negro wanting to get
into a country club. Charlie says they need to talk. Tshembe reveals that he was the revolutionary Kumalo's second-in-command
until he was removed for not having enough passion for the freedom movement, and he insists that they refer to each other for-
mally as "Mr." during their conversation. He says leaders like
Kumalo are visionaries, but their underlings are just trying to se-

cure positions for themselves when independence comes. Charlie cynically likens them to whites. Charlie tells of his first glimpse of black men when he was a child in Nebraska. He says that whites and blacks need to stop avoiding contact and really look at each other, build bridges to transcend governments and even race. Tshembe ridicules Charlie's naiveté and says that the scares in the African hills where his country's riches were mined are too hard to overcome for the sake of his dream of bridges, and he likens those scares to everything associated with the Mission. Charlie dismisses Tshembe's disgust with imperialism and his lack of appreciation for the sacrifice made by the people who run the Mission, the people who taught him to read and write. Charlie accuses him of hating all white men, to which Tshembe laughs saying that he wishes he could. But it is all more complex than that, for as he's seen in the West with its myriad cruelties to its own people, those who raided Africa for centuries never loved white men, either. Charlie accuses him of being a communist. Tshembe tells Charlie that his sentimental journey home was a mistake, that he longs to be with his European wife and child in England, and that not all black men have the deep and pure answers that Charlie seeks. Ngago brings Tshembe a message on a piece of bark which he looks at while speculating that his is the same problem faced by Orestes and Hamlet--there are so many things he'd rather be doing. The Woman with the spear appears, and Tshembe becomes transfixed saying that soon "she" will come for him. But he resists her, not wanting to participate in the destiny of his people. He cries to her urgings that he is not responsible, that he has "renounced all spears."

Act II, Scene 1: Two days later in the mid-morning outside, Marta and Charlie are wrapping bottles of drugs and covering them in leaves to keep them cool. She wonders why Reverend Neilsen has not returned. Charlie asks Marta questions about her professional and personal life and wonders, to Marta's irritation, if the Reverend Neilsen hasn't "capitalized" on the Mission and the sacrifices of others. She says that Tshembe's opinions (or those of the other blacks) don't count because they haven't earned the right to criticize yet, and she recalls the recent murder of the family by terrorists. She refuses to tell Charlie who Eric's father is.

Act II, Scene 2: Shortly after the preceding scene, Tshembe
is in a hut looking at a box of Eric's belongings. Eric enters
drunk and they talk, Tshembe noting Eric's little mirror.
Tshembe assumes that it was a gift from DeKoven as he grabs
Eric's bag and discovers women's makeup. Tshembe mocks
Eric's homosexuality, suggesting that he has become a victim,
and tells him that he should return to England with him. Charlie
enters the hut as Eric leaves. He and Tshembe have a drink of
whiskey he has brought with him. Tshembe says he plans to go
into the textile business, and Charlie tells him that Major Rice's
suggestion that he could do something for his people was true.
Charlie encourages him to use his influence with Kumalo to get
the leader to denounce terrorism. Tshembe remarks that without
the threat of violence, the whites won't talk of peace and freedom
for Africa. Tshembe says it's too late for non-violence and that
Charlie, like other whites, sees him merely as part of a mass of
"the blacks." Charlie accuses him of wanting vengeance, and
Tshembe says that racism, like religion, is a device to justify the
rule of some men over others. Charlie angrily chastises Tshembe
for not recognizing that they both want the same things, particularly when Tshembe refuses to respect his feelings or the work of
the hospital. Tshembe says they all want things at Africa's expense. Charlie leaves as Peter and Ngago (who carries a spear)
approach. Peter, revealing his secret, revolutionary self, asks
Tshembe why he did not answer the summons of the Council he
received the day before. Peter (who in such circumstances wishes
to be called Ntali, his African name) exhorts Tshembe to become
one of their people's leaders, while Tshembe says he's no longer
one of them, only a man. Peter reminds him of the parable of the
elephants and the hyenas, the latter losing their land because they
tried to reason out their differences instead of acting, like the elephants. He accuses Tshembe of being too full of what the Europeans have. He tells Tshembe that his father supported, indeed
conceived, the fight for freedom. Peter says the group meets
within an hour and Tshembe cries that he's not interested in killing anyone, particularly old missionaries. Peter expresses con-
tempt for Kumalo's wish to negotiate with the whites, suggesting
that the black leader will become the new overseer. He says that
all whites must be driven out. Tshembe says he will talk to Ku-

malo about the people's frustrations, and that they demand total black rule in one season. As Peter and Ngago leave, Abioseh approaches. Peter remarks to Tshembe that they won't try to recruit his brother--that they don't recruit "Europeans."

Act II, Scene 3: Late that afternoon, there is a sudden burst of voices, Major Rice insisting to DeKoven, who rushes in with a sick child in his arms, that the martial law measures are appropriate. Rice tells Charlie that authority in the colony has always depended upon the sacredness of white life and shudders to think what would happen if millions of blacks decided to start killing white men. He informs Madame and the rest that he is taking full command of the area since Kumalo has been arrested on a charge of conspiracy. Charlie says that the one man who offered hope for peace has been put in jail. Marta defends Rice. He tells Madame that he has to quarter his troops at the Mission. Madame resists, but DeKoven mockingly agrees that, as whites, they must cooperate. Rice then calls Peter over to him and, for Charlie's sake, demonstrates how Peter is an example of the whites' civilizing influences. Peter acts slavish and mouths the platitudes that Rice wants to hear, and Rice tells Charlie to write about such successes. Charlie encourages Madame to issue a statement in her husband's name to try and quell the tensions. She refuses to do so in his absence and wants to go to bed. Tshembe enters dressed in a suit and is looking for Major Rice. He wants an escort to take him to meet with Kumalo, but is told that he is too late; Kumalo has been arrested. Charlie says he'll do everything he can to help.

Act II, Scene 4: At noon the next day, Abioseh sits in the hut reading the Bible. Eric comes in for old Abioseh's shield and spear, but Abioseh tries to talk him out of joining the fight against the whites. Tshembe enters asking Eric which part of his half European self he will drive into the sea. The older brothers keep the boy from going and argue as to which one will take care of Eric. Tshembe mocks Abioseh's idea of Eric becoming a priest. Eric runs off after saying that Peter has asked him to join the revolutionaries. Abioseh says that people like Peter must be stopped because they make it impossible for responsible, practical men to exercise control. He envisions a time when all races live reasonably and peacefully together. He responds to Tshembe that he is not a Judas to his people, that he chose Africa while Tshembe sold himself to Europe. He berates Tshembe for believing in and acting on nothing. Abioseh says he's going to report Peter to Major Rice and leaves to do so over Tshembe's protests.

Act II, Scene 5: About an hour later Charlie is typing and complaining that there is no contact with the outside world. Tshembe arrives asking for Peter who, DeKoven says, has gone across the river. He sits and waits for him while DeKoven tells Charlie that the whites have tried to keep the blacks from entering the Twentieth Century. As a doctor, he says, he has saved lives to provide a rationale for genocide. He goes on to tell how the people changed from being passive under their white rulers seven years before. They came to Reverend Neilsen, led by Old Abioseh, with a petition requesting that the government grant them a constitution and representation. The Reverend patronizingly told his "children" to go home to their huts before they made him angry. Tshembe is moved by this story about his father's revolt for freedom. DeKoven says the whites must allow the coming tide of freedom or die. Charlie says what he has speculated, that Eric is the Reverend's son with Old Abioseh's wife. DeKoven corrects Charlie saying that Rice is Eric's father. Peter arrives as Rice, his soldiers, and Abioseh enter with the news that Reverend Neilsen has been killed and mutilated in a raid by blacks. Rice says a decisive white offensive will begin, and jets are heard overhead. As Rice is served by him, he refers to Peter as Ntali. Peter runs and is killed by Rice and his troops. They and Abioseh leave as Tshembe sinks to his knees beside the dead Peter.

Act II, Scene 6: It is the following day and Ngago, "the poet-warrior invoking the soul of his people," is dressed in fatigues and armed with a rifle as are other soldier/warriors. He speaks of the atrocities their people have suffered as jets and helicopters sound overhead. He exhorts them to "kill the invader."

Act II, Scene 7: It is sunset at the Mission and Charlie, preparing to leave, expresses his condolences to Madame. He meets Tshembe who mocks what he feels is Charlie's plan to write of how the blacks have responded with ingratitude to white attempts to civilize and help them. Charlie responds by pointing out Tshembe's hypocrisy, asking him if he will be running back to

Europe. With the noise of a helicopter blaring overhead, they shake hands and part.

Act II, Scene 8: Immediately following, Tshembe and Madame are sitting together. She reminisces about the early days when she and the Reverend arrived in Africa and says she will die in her adoptive home. She explains why the Reverend let Tshembe's mother die, saying he believed that her son, Eric, was a sin against God and His order which called for the separation of the races. Tshembe tearfully says he'd love to be in England with his family, but admits he knows he must stay and help his people. And she tells him to do it, that his country needs warriors like his father. He leaves as Abioseh enters.

Act II, Scene 9: It is night and Abioseh and Madame are near the Reverend's coffin. He tells her, and wants her to say, that he did the right thing in reporting Peter. Tshembe enters, wearing the robe his father had last worn to the Mission, and puts his hand on Madame's shoulder. Abioseh senses his presence and backs away, only to be stopped by warriors, Eric among them. Tshembe takes out a pistol and kills Abioseh. Then a soldier enters shooting wildly and the warriors open fire. Madame is accidentally killed. Tshembe catches her as she falls and, as the warriors run off, Eric throws a grenade into the Mission causing it to explode in flames. As Tshembe emits a cry of grief, The Woman appears.

Productions and Credits -- Broadway: Longacre Theatre, New York City, November 15, 1970. 40 performances. Final text adapted by Robert Nemiroff.

    Producer: Konrad Matthaei
    Director: John Berry
    Scenery: Peter Larkin
    Costumes: Jane Greenwood
    Lighting: Neil Peter Jampolis
    Ritual: Louis Johnson
    Sound: Jack Shearing
    Script Associate: Charlotte Zaltzberg
    Cast: Tshembe Matoseh -- James Earl Jones
          Charlie Morris -- Cameron Mitchell
          Abioseh Matoseh -- Earle Hyman

Madame Neilsen -- Lili Darvas
Eric -- Harold Scott
Major George Rice -- Ralph Purdom
Dr. Willy DeKoven -- Humbert Allen Astredo
Dr. Marta Gotterling -- Marie Andrews
Peter -- Clebert Ford
Warrior -- Charles Moore
Witch Doctor -- Joan Derby
First African -- Dennis Tate
Second African -- George Fairly
Third African -- William Ware
African Child -- Gregory Beyer
First Soldier -- Garry Mitchell
Second Soldier - Gwyllum Evans
Drummers -- Ladji Camara, Charles Payne

Reviews (play) -- R109-R131.

Other Secondary Sources -- S31, S33, S48, S63, S69, S79, S87, S112, S128, S130, S138, S139, S140, S144.

Critical Overview -- Hansberry began writing *Les Blancs* in 1960, continuing to work on it until her death in 1964. On November 15, 1970, it was produced at the Longacre Theatre by Robert Nemiroff, who reworked and adapted what she had left behind. He referred to the play as the "first major work by a black American playwright to focus on Africa and the struggle for black liberation" (S79). The drama grew out of her life-long interest in and study of continental African culture and history as well as her dissatisfaction with Jean Genet's *Les Negres* (*The Blacks*, 1960) which Hansberry felt did a weak job of portraying its characters as believable human beings (S79).

One of Hansberry's most controversial plays, *Les Blancs* was also one of her least successful, running for only forty-seven performances. Some thought it a passionate, moving expression of the complexities, frustrations, and realities of revolutionary times in Africa, while others felt it was a call for violent racial warfare.

Scholars have found *Les Blancs* a fascinating example of the breadth of Hansberry's talent as a playwright as well as the depth of her intellect. Gruesser (S138) notes the play is an attempt to "explode the dominant image of Africa by rewriting Joseph Conrad's *Heart of Darkness.*" And Ness (S33) writes in the same vein when he cites the play as being one about Tshembe's change to a commitment to his people, "one of the most profound and heroic victories of our modern literature." When he kills his brother, Abioseh, "who represents a slave-like service of the interests of the exploiters" of Africa and Africans, Tshembe is victorious in "making peace with the forces that live and grow by destroying his people."

In regard to Tshembe, Carter (S128) focuses on *Les Blancs'* similarities to Shakespeare's *Hamlet,* for both Hamlet and Tshembe have returned from abroad to attend their fathers' funerals and are confronted with spirits who call them to action to rectify injustices. Like Hamlet, also, Carter notes, the intellectual Tshembe is slow to commit himself and perform his duties, causing some loss of innocent life in the process. And while Hamlet agonizes over the immoral relationship his mother has with his stepfather, Tshembe perhaps grieves over the sex forced on his mother by Major Rice, Rice's supposed "rape" of her symbolizing the "rape" of an entire continent by white imperialists. Indeed, Eric, his homosexual, alcoholic half brother, is referred to as "the testament to three centuries of rape and self-acquittal."

As a political play, Cheney (S87) argues that *Les Blancs* is a call to "action and commitment" and a plea for the creation of a new Africa. And as such, Carter (S112) says it is "one of the most scathing and enduring indictments of colonialism and all similar social injustices, both from a European and African standpoint."

Cheney (S87) also notes Hansberry's finesse in underpinning the realistic drama of *Les Blancs* with Old African myths that signify profound rites of passage through which both Africans and their emerging countries must proceed. Not only do *death* and *initiation* rites add depth and deep human and cultural significance to Tshembe's experience, but the mystical and beautiful Woman who appears in the play reminds him, and the audience, of his primal heritage.

Wilkerson (S140) finds Tshembe to be an "articulate" character who "eloquently sets forth the reasons why his people cannot wait for freedom but who at the same time hesitates to join the revolution," while Adams (S79), agreeing that Tshembe is the most fully developed character in the play, laments the fact that the drama consists almost entirely of "humorless conversations about political and moral issues with little success in making the speakers come alive."

However, theatrical reviews of *Les Blancs* demonstrate that some of Hansberry's ideas struck emotional cords in her audience. While, according to Nemiroff (P2), some criticized the play for its "dullness and didacticism," one reviewer accurately reported that the opening night audience "responded violently" by clapping for either the whites' point of view or that of the blacks', "one black militant" having to be removed from the theater. Kerr (R113) dubbed the play a "mature work," its gaps compensated for by "the candor and drive of the play's speech, speech that might have been mere rhetoric but instead achieves a stage quickness." And Clurman (R115) insisted that the drama was "not propaganda, as has been inferred...but a forceful and intelligent statement of the tragic impasse of white and black relations all over the world." *Les Blancs*, he concludes, transcends the banalities of intellectual disputes and racial conflicts and "clarifies, but does not seek to resolve, the historical and human problems involved."

On the other hand, Barnes (R110) found *Les Blancs* shallow, "the arguments" all having been heard before and presented in a simplistic fashion. The "people in the play are debased puppets mouthing thoughts, hopes and fears that lace the surprise and vitality of life." Likewise, Kraus (R121) found that the play "never progressed beyond its primary stating of universal racial conflicts," or "repeating its rather obvious philosophical confusions." And Rudin (R118) chided the drama's "stretchiness, its awkwardness, its sometimes trenchant but too often cliché-ridden dialogue," concluding that Hansberry had not worked over her material sufficiently "to make the play transcend its now dated, familiar vision of the inevitability of black-white conflict."

Finally, however, Riley (R114) expressed the feelings of many blacks when he said that while *Les Blancs* may not be a "great piece of theater," it is, nonetheless, an "incredibly moving experience" of "ugliness recognized, filth and perversity definitely perceived, in that social order most people will recognize under its formal title--Western Civilization." As Hayman (R130) put it, the play is driven by "the fury of black nationalism," Hansberry's characters seeing a "long-standing social system...built on the oppressive but well-intended notion of White Man's Burden--crumble around them."

THE DRINKING GOURD (published 1972). P2

The Characters -- THE SOLDIER, a thoughtful American and narrator; RISSA, a slave cook and mother of Hannibal; HANNIBAL, a field slave of about nineteen or twenty, lean and vital, who has learned to read and write; SARAH, a slave girl of nineteen who loves Hannibal; HIRAM SWEET, in his mid sixties, the old master of the plantation who suffers from a heart condition; MARIA, Hiram's patient wife; EVERETT, Hiram's arrogant son who succeeds him as master; DR. MACON BULLETT, a southern aristocrat and Hiram's doctor; ZED DUDLEY, a "poor white" who becomes overseer for Everett; ELIZABETH DUDLEY, his wife; COFFIN, a black slave driver hated by the other slaves; TOMMY SWEET, the younger son of Hiram who has taught Hannibal to read and write; THE PREACHER, who tells Zeb that slavery has ruined the land; JOSHUA, a small slave boy of seven or eight, the son of Hannibal's brother, Isaiah, who has escaped to the North; TWO MALE HOUSE SERVANTS; TWO DUDLEY CHILDREN; A DRIVER; SLAVES--MEN, WOMEN, CHILDREN.

Plot Summary -- Prologue: Seated in a tiny, wooden enclosure, Hannibal is playing the banjo as Tommy Sweet keeps time with the music.

Act I: On the East Coast at dusk, the soldier/narrator says that Europe, Africa, the New World, and cotton have all "gotten mixed up together to make trouble." Voices sing the hymn "Steal away to Jesus," as the narrator describes how labor is so plentiful in the South that it might be cheaper to work a man to death and then buy another rather than to treat him less harshly so he will last. The words "quittin' time" are heard and the narrator points to the exhausted slaves as they file silently to their quarters. The narrator describes the horrors of the slave trade that brought the slaves to America. He notes that there are harsh laws to keep slaves from being educated. He reminds the audience that this is the Nineteenth Century, when child labor in the North is the norm, women are not considered equal citizens, and the mentally ill are punished for their madness. The scene changes. The slaves are seen getting their meal from Rissa, an older slave woman. Sarah plays with a child, Joshua, who says he has a stomach ache. She teases with him. Rissa tells them to stop it, and Sarah asks where Hannibal is. Rissa says she does not know where her wild son is. Sarah tells Rissa that Hannibal had sneaked out of the fields again and that Coffin, the black slave driver, was going to report this to Master Sweet. Rissa gives Sarah some supper for Hannibal, and she goes to a hill where he lies on his back looking at the stars. He recites some romantic poetry, and pulls her down to kiss her. He laughs at the news that Coffin noticed he had gone off. He says they were "born in trouble" with the Master. He has her gaze at the big dipper, the "Drinkin' Gourd," which points straight to the North Star. He speculates that the stars would provide good traveling light tonight as she tries to hush such frightful talk of the dream of escape. He sings a freedom hymn as Sara compares him to his brother, who escaped to the North. Hannibal tells her he knows his brother, Isaiah, is alive. She recollects how Isaiah went out of his head when his wife was sold, causing him to leave his son, Joshua, behind and go to secure his own freedom and then that of his wife and take her to the North. Hannibal tells her he would like to escape, as well. Sarah is frightened at the prospect, and he tells her he will come back and buy her and his mother. The scene changes to the "Big House," where Hiram Sweet and his family are finishing their meal with their guest, Dr. Macon Bullett. Everett says the South has plenty of men and would win a war with the North in six months. His father disagrees, and Dr. Bullett says that war is inevitable, that every Yankee industrialist fancies himself the deliverer of the slaves. All they want in reality, he says, is control of Congress. To his serious son's dismay, Hiram says the South couldn't win the war, asking him who would keep the slaves on the plantations if the southern white men were off fighting. Hiram points out

how more and more slaves are running off as it is. He says he
believes in slavery, but that it's serious business that may decide
the course of a war and the winner of it. When Everett says if it
became necessary, the South could arm the blacks, Hiram mocks
Everett's naiveté at thinking blacks would fight for something
they are trying to run away from. Everett and his father argue,
Hiram saying that his son won't be running the plantation until he
can do it in his father's humane "tradition." Everett labels his
father old-fashioned. Then Dr. Bullett says he must get on with
his examination of Hiram, who has a bad heart. Maria tries to
clam people down, and Everett resents being treated like a child.
Hiram recollects how he started his plantation with only $50 and
four slaves. Everett suggests again that times have changed and
plantations should be run differently these days. Hiram mocks the
"modern" way of doing it: putting everything in the hands of
overseers. Everett points out some realities about the decreasing
profitability of the plantation. Hiram admits the land is about
finished, and that they need new acreage and more slaves. And
since the African slave trade is forbidden, slaves are too expen-
sive. Everett calls the plantation under his father's control a
"resort for slaves" and insists that they must somehow up the
yield or go bankrupt. The way to do it, he says to his father who
thinks nine hours of work a day for the slaves is enough, is to
keep them in the fields longer. Maria calms them down, and after
she leaves the room Dr. Bullett tells Hiram that he can no longer
do much more than read, that his physical condition is that bad.
Dr. Bullett recommends that Hiram turn his plantation over to his
son. Hiram mentions his "gray hours," when he wonders why
there are stars and why he lives at all. He worries about being
judged ill by God for owning slaves. They all exit except Hiram
who is joined by Rissa. She calls him stubborn, and he again
recollects how he came with only a little money and a few slaves
(one of whom was Rissa) and built a fine plantation. He also laments that one of the four, Ezekiel, ran off. They reminisce about
by-gone days and experiences they had together. At his request,
she gets him his old rifle to hold. Rissa reminds him of his promise to make Hannibal a house slave. He says that he will keep his
promise as soon as picking season is over. His wife, who has entered and overheard this, is angry at this, and Hiram explodes,

saying that he will do as he wishes as Master and will not die curled up with a book!

Act II: Everett is sitting alone, dejected and drinking, when his mother bursts in with the news that his father has had an attack. The scene changes to Hiram's bedroom where Maria is calming her delirious husband. She insists to Everett that he take over as master of the plantation, but to just let his father "think" that he is still running things. The scene changes to the poor farm of Zeb Dudley. The preacher arrives. Zeb tells him despairingly that he's getting ready to clear out and maybe head to the West. Zeb tells the preacher that if he had slaves he could make a life for himself. He calls his father a fool for not owning slaves, but the preacher disagrees. Everett Sweet arrives and offers Zeb the job of overseer on his plantation, and he accepts. The preacher finds it sad and says that men's hands were not meant to crack whips on other men's backs. He says cotton and slavery have ruined the land. Zeb says that his goal is to own slaves to do his work for him, and the preacher asks for God's mercy on all. The scene changes to Rissa's cabin, late in the evening. Slaves are in a circle singing the illegal song, "Raise a Ruckus." Coffin scolds the other slaves for singing the song and warns them of the consequences. Rissa dismisses him, but Coffin says he wants to speak to Hannibal. He questions Hannibal about running off during the day when he is supposed to be picking cotton and asks Rissa to deal with her son in this regard. Hannibal mocks him, and Coffin warns him to stop sassing. Coffin says Hannibal should work hard, and Hannibal retorts the fields aren't his. After Coffin leaves, Rissa asks her son why he runs off all the time and then accuses him of stealing the master's Bible. Rissa is afraid Hannibal won't be permitted to work in the Big House if he continues to misbehave, but he says he doesn't want to work there anyway. She counsels him to do his work and appreciate being a slave of such a benevolent master as Hiram Sweet. He says he plans to be a bad slave and pretend, whenever he can, to be lazy instead of quick, sick instead of healthy, and stupid instead of smart. He says, the more pain this behavior costs the master, the more Hannibal is a man. He then calms down and tells his mother he can read, and that's why he stole the Bible. When he shows her he can, she is pleased that she has a boy who can read the Scriptures. He tells her he's also learning to write, but he won't tell her who is teaching him. She recalls how both a black man who learned to read and the white man who taught him were punished for their crimes. She tells him he must quit, and he leaves telling her that it's too late for her, she can only think like a slave. The scene changes to the fields in the morning. Zeb is telling the drivers that the working hours of the slaves are to be extended. A driver tries to talk Zeb out of his plans, but to no avail. Coffin agrees with Zeb, and goes on to tell him about Hannibal's running off. When he sees Hannibal, Zeb questions him about his brother who ran off and then whips him across the face as an example to the other slaves. They all continue work. The scene changes to the verandah of the Big House. Everett is telling Zeb to take care who he picks to punish, that his father holds Rissa and her children with affection. He also reminds Zeb that he is the master and everyone, including Zeb, will do as he says. Coffin arrives with the report that Hannibal has run off again. He shocks them by reporting that Hannibal is with young Tommy, and he leads them there. The scene changes, and Tommy is practicing playing the banjo and taking instructions from Hannibal. Tommy then gives Hannibal his writing lesson, as he had promised. He looks at Hannibal's story called "The Drinking Gourd." Hannibal asks Tommy to read it out loud, which he does. Tommy corrects Hannibal's primitive mistakes as he reads the "story" about how looking at the stars conjures the feeling of freedom. Then Everett, Zeb, and Coffin arrive. Tommy is sent home. Everett gets Hannibal to admit what Tommy has taught him. He looks into Hannibal's eyes, which makes him think of the only thing to do to punish an educated slave. As the Bible says, one must cut out the diseased part of the body, and a slave's ability to read is a disease. Hannibal, not realizing the cruelty they are capable of, says that they can never take away his ability to read and write no matter how hard they beat him. Everett demands that Hannibal's eyes be put out and tells the horrified Zeb to do it. As Everett leaves, Hannibal's screams of agony are heard.

Act III: Late night on the plantation grounds, two voices are heard remarking that they might as well cut Hannibal down from where he's tied between trees now, that gangrene must have set in. The scene changes to the interior of Hiram Sweet's bedroom

where Hiram is angrily denouncing Zeb and Everett. He tells Zeb
to get off his land before he shoots him. Zeb leaves as Dr. Bullett
arrives with the news that the Civil War has begun with the firing
on Fort Sumter two days before. He and Everett cry out with joy
for the South. Soberly, Hiram calls them fools and says that the
South is lost. Whoever fired on Sumter freed the slaves and destroyed a way of life. Hiram predicts the blacks will be armed by
the North to fight against their oppressors. Then, over the protests of Dr. Bullett, he leaves to see Rissa. As he goes, he says he
believed in slavery, but that he also understood it. He might as
well die with it. The scene changes to the exterior of Rissa's
cabin. Hiram enters to see Rissa at the fire boiling something,
and Hannibal lying on his back with his eyes covered. Hiram, in
pain himself, says he'll send for Dr. Bullett to tend to Hannibal,
but Rissa says she can doctor him, asking if Bullett can put Hannibal's eyes back in. Hiram tells her he had nothing to do with
the blinding, but she asks if he is or is not the master? When he
objects to her tone, she asks if the overseer will put her eyes out,
too. She says she wouldn't care; she's seen enough of this world.
Hiram leaves dejectedly, and once outside the cabin falls in pain.
He calls for help, but Rissa methodically tends to her son and ig-
nores Hiram's cries until they stop completely. The scene
changes to the verandah of the Big House in the evening. Maria
is dressed in black, and Everett is in a Confederate uniform.
Everett tries to console his mother, but she refuses to go for a ride
or cheer up. From the slave quarters they can hear the slaves
singing "Steal Away to Jesus," and Everett remarks how pretty it
is. He says it's peaceful, and when she questions that characterization of the mood of things, he says that Zeb is running the
plantation well and that everything is very orderly and disciplined.
He also says that the war will be over soon, he'll be back, and
things will be even better. The scene changes to Rissa. She is
taking Hiram's gun from its cabinet. She exits out the kitchen
and, with Joshua, heads to the woods where she meets the pensive
Sarah and her blind son. She gives the gun and the child's hand
to Sarah and then, after an embrace, watches the three go off into
the woods toward freedom as the singing of "The Drinking
Gourd" is heard. The scene changes to the Soldier/Narrator who,
in the deserted slave quarters, is in a Union uniform. He says that

slavery is a drag on the development of a great industrial nation, that we can't let it destroy the union which our founding fathers envisioned, and that it has already cost us, as a nation, too much of our soul. The war, it is suggested, is inevitable for the good of all.

Secondary Sources -- S31, S46, S51, S52, S69, S72, S79, S87, S88, S93, S98, S128, S130, S140, S146.

Critical Overview -- In 1960, *The Drinking Gourd* was commissioned by NBC television to be a part of a series of plays commemorating the centennial of the Civil War, but the play was never produced. Although producer Dore Schary said Hansberry's was a "powerful and marvelous script that might have been...one of the great things we've seen on television," it was finally rejected, perhaps for not expressing the "Gone With the Wind" variety of the war and slavery that network executives had envisioned. Equally disturbing to them, Robert Nemiroff (P2) has said, was the fact that Hansberry treated whites and blacks objectively; both were victimized physically and psychologically by the institution of slavery. Horrible enough was the fact of the black hero's blinding for learning how to read, but Hansberry also insisted on empathizing as well with the *white* forced to blind him. In 1965, efforts were under way again to produce the play which would star Claudia McNeil, Fredric March, and Florence Eldridge, but this time, it was CBS which refused, claiming the drama was not "contemporary" enough and that blacks did not want "to be reminded that they were once slaves" (S79).

Scholarly work on the play has been limited. Most, like Cheney (S87) find the premise of the drama to be that institutions, "unlike the individuals in them--are evil and all-consuming." Also, Hannibal's experience demonstrates clearly that the white man's power to enslave the black man has as its foundation "the denial of literacy." His penalty for learning how to read, Cheney (S87) concludes, "becomes both a literal and symbolic punishment. He will still prevail, for young Joshua, biblical namesake of the leader of the Promised Land, guides Hannibal and Sarah to freedom." Carter (S128) sees the play as a "highly-charged study of three levels of antebellum Southern society--planters, slaves,

and poor whites." And he agrees with Nemiroff that Hansberry's
object "was not to pose black against white, to create black heroes and white villains, but to locate the sources of human behavior, of both heroism and villainy, *within* the slave society." Wilkerson (S72) finds it significant that Hansberry dramatizes the
slave's rejection of white authority in the character of Rissa, a
woman. By having her tend her blinded son rather than help the
dying Hiram, who is as much her friend as master, the playwright
debunks the myth of the "forgiving, master-loving slave woman,"
of the *Gone With the Wind* tradition. As Miller (S51) suggests,
Rissa is a real human capable of kindness as well as revenge
when it comes to the treatment of her family. And in this, as
Friedman (S88) notes, she parallels black women of modern
times. She focuses on Rissa from a feminist viewpoint, finding
her, as well as Lena of *A Raisin in the Sun*, to be images of black
women who *do not* emasculate black men. Rather, they are
women "who contribute not only to the survival of their families
and communities, but also to the active resistance often necessary
to that survival."

WHAT USE ARE FLOWERS (published 1972). P2

The Characters -- HERMIT, Charles Lewis Lawson, a seventy-
eight-year-old former English professor who has lived in the
woods by himself for twenty years; CHARLIE, an intelligent
child most sensitive to the hermit's teachings; LILY, the only girl
child; CHILDREN, the other seven or so children, none beyond
the age of ten, who, along with Charlie and Lily, the hermit tries
to teach.

Plot Summary -- Scene 1: In the darkness a hermit appears and goes
to sleep in a small cave. Nine or ten wild-looking children appear
hunting some small creature. As the light of dawn intensifies, the
children stone and kill the animal they are stalking, and the
strongest among them begins to eat it raw. The sounds they make
wake the hermit who startles them when he remarks disdainfully
on their animalistic behavior. He moves toward the fearful children asking them for assistance. He remarks their lack of man-

ners but says, with their race, manners only disguise greater crimes, anyway. He regrets that the first humans he sees in twenty years are abusing an animal. The children continue to stare as he tries to ask them the way to a city, to "civilization." He speculates that their primitive appearances might be due to it being Halloween. He tells them he'd like to know what time it is, and tells them how the compulsion to escape time that led him to the forest was always accompanied by the urge to know the correct time and date. He says men don't make time, but they can give it its worthless, important, or absurd dimensions. He says it's time for him to die, and that he is returning contemptuously to society to see what mankind has been doing. The children continue to stare in silence. Irritated, he tells them to go away so he can eat his breakfast, but they appear not to understand him. As he begins to eat, the children, like animals, lunge for his food. He chastises them and leaves to find the city on his own, only to return. He tries to encourage them to tell him how to get to the town and frightens them when he starts a fire with a flint. While fearing the fire, the children come closer when they smell the wild fowl he begins to cook. They throw themselves on the birds and devour them. With this, the hermit realizes that they are not pretending, they *are* wild and cannot understand language. He screams at civilization, "What have you done?"

Scene 2: Many weeks later the children sit in a semicircle with the hermit standing in front of them in the role of teacher. He names them all. He calls their attention to certain objects and actions, and the children repeat the appropriate words for them. He then moves to show them how to make clay pots to use for carrying things. He uses the pot he has made to teach them the concept of "use," and Charlie seems to understand. He moves on to show them the skill of weaving.

Scene 3: Stone implements, drying food, and baskets show the growth of civilization. The boys have had their hair cut, the girl's being left long. The hermit compliments them on how quickly they are learning. He says he and Charlie have a "surprise" for the rest of the children, something experienced by nose, eyes, "and way deep inside you": *beauty.* The children repeat the word. One of the boys asks what the use of flowers is. He tells them how they can smell, touch, and write verses about them. He then begins to sing "Greensleeves" to them as an example of melody and music. Then Charlie surprises the other children by playing the melody on a crude flute. The hermit finally gets them all to sing to the music of the flute. The girl, Lily, asks what the use of music is. The hermit, referring to Beethoven's Ninth, says there are many uses.

Scene 4: In the darkness comes the sound of Charlie's flute playing the Choral of Beethoven's Ninth. The hermit is very pleased. The children sing in a crude chorus, the hermit directing. He then talks to Charlie alone and tries to teach the boy to converse. He tells Charlie that he (Charlie) is the children's leader and attempts to explain the significance of Lily's sexuality to him, that he and she might be responsible for the survival of the race. In the meantime, two of the boys get in a fight over one of them trying to steal some of the other's pots. The hermit is bitterly angry at them and, as they continue to fight, calls them animals who do not deserve to survive.

Scene 5: A few hours later, the hermit is on his back in his lean-to. The apprehensive children send Charlie to him with flowers. He tells Charlie that he hates the children, including Charlie, because they are human, and as such, repulsive. He has decided to die alone. The hermit tries to explain the awesomeness of death they will witness when he dies. He tells Charlie the children will have to bury him, and that he does not know the answer to the question of immortality. He says the children will miss him and discover the abstractions of "affection" and "grief," both based upon love. Charlie inquires as to the use of "love." The hermit asks Charlie if he likes Lily and worries that all the boys will want her someday. He says Charlie must protect the health and well-being of Lily at all costs. Then the hermit questions Charlie as to how the children got there in the first place, and Charlie tells him in gestures. The hermit interprets as the boy continues his "narrative" which relates how a big woman brought them there and kissed them goodbye. The hermit overcomes his cynicism and dubs the woman a hero. He tells the boy of how "valiant" the human race was when up against the reckless universe. Then, another boy enters and shows the hermit that he has made a water wheel. In a jealous rage, Charlie grabs the invention and throws it out of the lean-to. The hermit says that jealousy must not be used to selfishly destroy, but to improve things, to cooperatively make things better for all. However, he says he does not think they will learn this lesson, that all the great things of the civilization he had rejected are lost. As Charlie holds up the flower, the hermit, with his dying breath, says "the uses of flowers were infinite." Outside, the boy who had invented the wheel is reconstructing it as the other children watch.

Review -- R132.

Other Secondary Sources -- S31, S79, S87, S121, S128, S130, S140.

Critical Overview -- *What Use Are Flowers* was, like *The Drinking Gourd*, written for television. When it was also rejected by NBC, Hansberry reworked it into a play that was never professionally produced for the New York stage. It takes place some time after a nuclear holocaust and involves the efforts of a seventy-eight-year-old hermit's efforts to instill the positive aspects of civilization in a group of nine or ten children who also survived and have been living primitively animalistic lives. According to Nemiroff (P2), while the play has its similarities to William Golding's *Lord of the Flies*, Hansberry had not read that novel until a year after finishing *What Use Are Flowers*. Carter (S128) agrees with Nemiroff that the work was the playwright's response to the deeply pessimistic suggestions about the absurd nature of existence as she understood them to be expressed in Beckett's *Waiting For Godot*. As Nemiroff (P2) put it, the drama was "her answer to the questions of life and death, survival and absurdity which Beckett had posed in such novel and compelling terms." And it is in this vein that Wilkerson (S109) insists Hansberry's was, indeed, a vision which could simultaneously admit a sense of the meaninglessness and absurdity of existence, while at the same time celebrate the human race's frequent triumphs "if not nature, *over* the absurd." Yet Adams (S79) concludes, the drama is a weak answer to Beckett, "Hansberry's inevitable optimism" seeming strained when "she takes on nuclear destruction."

The "world premiere" production of *What Use Are Flowers* took place as part of the National Black Arts Festival in Atlanta

in 1994. In a pre-production review, Hulbert (R132) describes
the work as a "fable" which reveals Hansberry's "almost mystical
belief in the human spirit."

TOUSSAINT (Excerpt from Act I of a Work in Progress, published
1986). P10

The Characters -- BAYON DE BERGIER, the plantation manager,
in his middle fifties, who longs to return to Paris; LUCIE, his
Creole wife, in her late twenties or early thirties, who considers
Santo Domingo her home; DESTINE, Lucie's slave servant.

Plot Summary -- It is, presumably, early evening in the Great House
of a sugar plantation in Santo Domingo (Haiti) in the 1780's.
Bayon stands in unfinished dress while his wife reclines on a
cushioned chaise. Lucie tells her husband that she's not interested
in hearing what he and his guests will be saying about the plantation, crops, politics, or Napoleon. She finds such talk dull and
tiresome. He informs her that she *will* dress and listen to what
their guests have to say, and that she *will* use her best theatrical
talents to make them feel she enjoys and is interested in everything
they have to say. He sighs, and she says he sighs a great deal, of
late. He says he's very tired and has agonies. She mocks his
"agonies" as she picks up his muddy boots and, with irritation,
wonders why he no longer tries to hide his visits to his dead mistress's grave. When he did so, she still had a shred of love for
him, but no more. She questions if he still brings orange blos-
soms, and wonders if, when he puts them on the grave, a voice
calling him her "Ivory God" comes forth. Lucie is unmoved when
he violently grabs the boots and throws them across the room.
She looks at the mountains and asks what made him bury her up
there. She affects the mannerisms of the dying slave/lover and
asks if she begged him to bury her there. He says there is nothing
for him to say. He tells her if she wishes to torture herself, he will
not help her. She says he'd loved to have married his lover, but
that she needs to learn to pretend not to suffer like the other wives
in Santo Domingo. Bayon says that they will forget about it when
they are home in France, but she says that she *is* home now be-

cause she is a Creole. She says she intends to die in Santo Domingo, and he mocks her romantic notions. She changes the subject and asks about the Petions, who will be their guests. He dresses and looks for the garters she has playfully hidden while describing Mr. Petion. Marcel Petion is the courier of his employer, Bayon says, having found the hidden garters and continuing to dress. He wants the courier, who is going to survey the plantation for its owner in France, to write a good report so he can remain in charge of the plantation for one more year. Petion, therefore, must be well-entertained. She mockingly concludes that, after one more year, it is Bayon's plan that they will then go live in Paris, and he confirms this. She ridicules him as a petit bourgeois who likes to sit astride his horse in the fields, play-acting at being the master when he is merely the manager. Furthermore, she says, the real owner is too occupied with court life in France to even bother to inspect the plantation for himself. Lucie attributes Bayon's irritation with her to the fact that she is a "Creole pig," and that he feels he married beneath himself. She castigates him for his past insults concerning her parentage and reiterates that he is an "affected little bourgeois worshipper of the aristocracy." He says he's sorry he has burdened her with his regrets about his not being able to marry into a distinguished family. She expresses her rage at having her family described as the "baggage of Paris gutters," and he tells her to stop talking. He asks for her forgiveness at saying such things, but she says she can't. She likens herself to a slave, a "creature purchased." They hear the crack of a whip and she asks who Toussaint is having punished now. She calls Toussaint a brute and wonders what would happen if he ever ran away. Bayon says that Toussaint, his plantation steward, never will, that he is given certain freedoms that make for his contentment. Bayon says Toussaint has his own "sense of the order of things." She remarks how strange it is for her husband to pretend to be in command of the plantation when, in reality, it is the slave Toussaint who is. Bayon explains that while Toussaint is not a slave he is not free, either. She asks her husband if he, himself, is free. With the sound of the whip, she speculates if Toussaint gets pleasure from the beating of the slaves. Bayon says he does, but she says she's witnessed his merciless way with the slaves and has seen no pleasure in it. Bayon says he's glad he has a steward who can "drive men," and then changes his phrase to "drive slaves." She asks the difference and then says that the expression she saw on Toussaint's face during a whipping he was overseeing was "the most complicated expression" she had ever observed. She speculates that Toussaint can command men as well as slaves, and perhaps even commands Bayon. He says that is untrue, that Toussaint is content; that he is a special kind of black who is strange and mystical in his acceptance of his fate; that he is a wise man. Lucie's servant arrives as Bayon leaves the room. Lucie reprimands her for being late to help her bathe. As Destine massages her while she bathes, Lucie speculates that the slaves will all run off some day and return with fire and machetes. She asks Destine if she despises her. When the servant says she does not, Lucie says that she, indeed, does--that she hates her white mistress. In a state, she slaps Destine and accuses her of wanting to murder her. She knows what slaves think because she is a Creole and can see it. All the slaves are waiting for their chance to rebel, Lucie says. Destine responds that she is waiting for nothing, that she is content. Lucie tells Destine harshly to finish the massage. With a change of mood, Lucie begins to admire Destine's beauty and caresses her. Bayon enters to get something and, with disgust, tells her to join their guests, *when she is finished.* As he exits, she screams after him that her pleasures are her own and remarks that nothing really matters. She has Destine continue to massage her.

Secondary Sources -- S3, S79, S87, S120, S128.

Critical Overview -- *Toussaint,* published as *Toussaint: Excerpt From Act I of a Work in Progress* (P10), was one of the scripts left unfinished at the time of Hansberry's death in 1965.   At various times conceived by the playwright as a musical, an opera, and a play, it has never been produced professionally on the New York stage (P2).   As far back as her grade school years, she identified Toussaint L'Ouverture as one of her heroes.   In fact, in Hansberry's "A Note to Readers" (P2) in the volume where the only published excerpt of the play appears, she says she was "obsessed with the idea of writing a play (or at the time even a novel) about the Haitian liberator...I thought that...[he] was one of

the most extraordinary personalities to pass through history."
Moreover, she considered that *Toussaint* might one day develop
into her most notable creation, "my epic work," as she put it (P2).
According to Carter (S128) one of the few critics to discuss it in
any detail, the published excerpt of *Toussaint* reveals some of
Hansberry's "finest dialogue, characterization, and development
of situation--concise, multilayered, and resonant." He goes on to
point out how the first act of her play, at one level, establishes the
characters as human beings, real people. The next level of the
play "connects these personal problems with representative problems of the time and place"--the social, economic, and political
milieu of the Caribbean island of Santo Domingo (Haiti) in the
1780's with its dependence on slavery which allowed sugar plantations to make profits for absentee landlords residing in France.
Also apparent in the play is the exploration of what Lloyd
Richards (P2), who directed the scene for a public television
broadcast, called "three levels of slavery": actual slaves, the
slavery of a woman to her unloving husband, and the slavery of
the master/manager to the system/institution of slavery. Carter
(S128) asserts that a further level of interest involves the conflict
between "opposing cultures of master and slave represented by
the background music, while a final dimension of the excerpt
provides information about Toussaint himself and the suggested
complexities of his character." As Hansberry (S120) herself said
in reference to *Toussaint*, an "oppressive society will dehumanize
and degenerate everyone involved," and it will at the same time
"tend to make the oppressed have more stature," because they are
"arbitrarily placed" in a situation of having to overwhelm "that
which is degenerate," in the case of *Toussaint*, the slave society.

Primary Bibliography: Writings by Hansberry

The following is an alphabetized collection of Hansberry's writings arranged as follows: I. Drama, II. Fiction and Poetry, III. Non-Fiction (selectively annotated), IV. Interviews, V. Media Productions, VI. Unpublished Materials, and VII. Archival Sources.

I. DRAMA

P1   *Lorraine Hansberry's "A Raisin in the Sun" and "The Sign in Sidney Brustein's Window."* Foreword by John Braine. New York: New American Library, 1966. Includes Robert Nemiroff's "The 101 'Final' Performances of *Sidney Brustein*." This edition restores cuts from the Broadway production of *A Raisin in the Sun* not included in many editions.

P2   *Lorraine Hansberry: The Collected Last Plays (Les Blancs, The Drinking Gourd, What Use Are Flowers?).* Edited with critical background by Robert Nemiroff. Introduction by Margaret B. Wilkerson. Foreword and afterword by Julius Lester. New York: New American Library, 1983. Restores some sequences cut from the Broadway production of *Les Blancs*.

P3   *Raisin.* New York: Samuel French, 1978. Musical.

P4   *A Raisin in the Sun.* New York: Random House, 1959; London: Metheun, 1960.

P5   *A Raisin in the Sun,* the complete, original version with new introduction by Robert Nemiroff. New York: Signet, 1988.

P6   *A Raisin in the Sun: The Unfilmed Original Screenplay.* New York: Plume/Penguin, 1992. Edited by Robert Nemiroff with Foreword by Jewell Handy Nemiroff, Introduction by Margaret B. Wilkerson, and Commentary by Spike Lee.

P7   *The Sign in Sidney Brustein's Window.* New York: Random House: 1965.

P8   *To Be Young, Gifted and Black: Lorraine Hansberry in Her Own Words.* Adapted by Robert Nemiroff. Englewood Cliffs, NJ: Prentice-Hall, 1969.

P9   *To Be Young, Gifted and Black: A Portrait of Lorraine Hansberry In Her Own Words* (acting edition). Adapted by Robert Nemiroff. New York: French, 1971.

P10   *"Toussaint:* Excerpt From a Work in Progress." In *Nine Plays by Black Women.* Edited by Margaret B. Wilkerson. New York: New American Library, 1986.

II. FICTION AND POETRY

FICTION

A1   "All the Dark and Beautiful Warriors." *Village Voice* 16 Aug. 1983: 1+.

A2   "The Buck Williams Tennessee Memorial Association." *Southern Exposure* Sept./Oct. 1984: 28-30. Excerpt from uncompleted novel.

POETRY

A3   "Lynchsong." *Masses & Mainstream* 4 (July 1951): 19-20.

A4   "Flag From a Kitchenette Window." *Masses & Mainstream* 3
        (Sept. 1950): 38-40.

III. NON-FICTION

B1   "American Theatre Needs Desegregating Too." *Negro Digest* 10
        (June 1961): 28-33.

B2   "An Author's Reflections: Willy Loman, Walter Younger, and
        He Who Must Live." *Village Voice* 12 Aug. 1959: 7-8.
        Reprinted in *The Village Voice Reader*, edited by Daniel
        Wolf and Edwin Fancher (New York: Doubleday, 1962);
        and in *Women in Theatre: Compassion and Hope*, ed-
        ited by Karen Malpede (New York: Drama Book, 1983).
                All in all, Hansberry says *A Raisin in the Sun*
        has been "magnificently understood." Compares Walter
        Lee to Willy Loman, noting they both share "the acute
        awareness that *something* is obstructing some abstract
        progress that they feel they should be making; that
        something is in the way of their 'ascendancy.'" It does
        not occur to either of them to "question the nature of this
        desired 'ascendancy.'"

B3   "The Black Revolution and the White Backlash." *National
        Guardian* 26 (4 July 1964): 5-9.

B4   "A Challenge to Artists." *Freedomways* 3 (Winter 1963): 33-35.
                A speech in which Hansberry insists artists who
        are lovers of freedom and committed to change must
        "paint," "sing," and "write" about their concerns even
        though it is "not currently fashionable" to do so.

B5   "Congolese Patriot." *New York Times Magazine* 26 March 1961:
        4. Letter to the Editor.

Hails the murdered Congolese patriot, Patrice
Lumumba, as a leader who will one day be regarded as
the "spiritual father" of an independent Congo Republic.
Insists that the "continuation of intrigues against African
and American Negro freedom demands high and steadfast
unity among Negroes."

B6   "The Creative Use of the Unconscious." *Journal of American
        Academy of Psychotherapists* 5 (1964): 13-17.

B7   "Images and Essences: 1961 Dialog with an Uncolored Egghead
        Containing Wholesome Intentions and Some Sass." *Ur-
        banite* 1 (May 1961): 10+.

B8   "The Legacy of W.E.B. Du Bois." *Freedomways* 5 (Winter
        1965): 19-20.

B9   "A Letter From Lorraine Hansberry on *Porgy and Bess.*" *Thea-
        tre* (Aug. 1959): 10.
                In terms of *Porgy and Bess*, Hansberry laments
        portrayals of blacks as "the hip-swinging, finger snapping
        race of prostitutes and pimps which people the imagina-
        tion of white writers of musical comedy 'Negro' shows,"
        or the "misguided desire of certain elements of the Negro
        middle class to see that particular horror replaced with
        well-heeled, suave, Oxfordian types."

B10   Letter signed L.N. *Ladder* 1.2 (1957): 26-30.
                An anonymous letter published in this lesbian
        journal in which Hansberry argues that homosexuals have
        experienced the same suppression as women, blacks, and
        others. Calls for a reexamination of society to instigate
        liberating change.

B11   "Letters from Readers: 'My Negro Problem'--11." *Commentary*
        May 1963: 430-31.
                Argues passionately that white liberals "ought be
        saying and doing *something*" for the cause of civil rights
        instead of looking for excuses not to do so.

B12   "Mailbag--'O'Casey--Hansberry.'" *New York Times* 28 June
        1959: 2.1:x3.

        Responds to an observation that *A Raisin in the
        Sun* "owes" much to Sean O'Casey's *Juno and the Pay-
        cock*, asserting that while she is indebted to O'Casey "in
        the spirit," her play accurately reflects characteristic
        "Negro life," albeit "'Junoesque'" to some.

B13   "Me Tink Me Hear Sounds in de Night." *Theatre Arts* 4 (Oct.
        1960): 9+. Reprinted as "The Negro in the American
        Theatre." *American Playwrights on Drama*. Ed. Horst
        Frenz. New York: Hill and Wang, 1965.

        Cultural history has produced a theater whose
        "dramatists are baffled by the Negro character, and
        whose producers and their receptionists are reduced to
        rudeness or apologetic embarrassment as they face the
        miraculously stubborn and increasing battalion of dark,
        hopeful faces among the multitude of other hopeful faces
        in their famous outer offices." Argues against the "color
        barrier" in the theater, whose essence "has always been
        illusion."

B14   "Miss Hansberry on 'Backlash.'" *Village Voice* 23 (July 1964):
        10+.

        Regrets a distorted assessment of a Town Hall
        Forum on "The Negro Revolution and the White Back-
        lash" which erroneously suggested there was a consensus
        of the black panelists present that, among other things,
        whites were merely "self-flagellating masochists of
        twisted Baldwin-built guilt who are incapable of assess-
        ing black villainy any more."

B15   *The Movement: Documentary of a Struggle for Equality*. New
        York: Simon and Schuster, 1964. Reprinted as *A Matter
        of Colour: Documentary of the Struggle for Racial
        Equality in the USA*. London: Penguin, 1965.

B16   "My Name is Lorraine Hansberry, I am a Writer." *Esquire* 72
        (Nov. 1969): 140.

B17   "The Nation Needs Your Gifts." *Negro Digest* 13 (Aug. 1964):
       26-29.
              Tells talented, black young people that they are
       "a product of a presently insurgent and historically viva-
       cious and heroic culture, a culture of indomitable will for
       freedom and aspiration to dignity."

B18   "The Negro in American Culture" (symposium with James
       Baldwin, Emile Capouya, Lorraine Hansberry, Nat Hen-
       toff, Langston Hughes, and Alfred Kazin). *Black Ameri-
       can Writer* 1: *Fiction*. Ed. C.W.E. Bigsby. Baltimore:
       Pelican Books, 1971.

B19   "Negro Writer and His Roots: Toward a New Romanticism."
       Black Scholar 12 (March-April 1981): 2-12.
              Hansberry's "artistic credo."   Among other
       things, asserts that "we are beset with the most funda-
       mental illusion...that art is not, and *should* not and, when
       it is as its best, CANNOT possibly be social." The at-
       tack of this "illusion is of vital importance to the Negro
       writer in particular."

B20   "Negroes and Africa." Hansberry is often quoted in this chapter
       in *The New World of Negro Americans*. Ed. Harold R.
       Isaacs. New York: Day, 1965.

B21   "Ocomogosiay!" *Black Collegian* 14 (March/April 1984): 48.

B22   "On Arthur Miller, Marilyn Monroe, and 'Guilt.'" *Women in
       Theatre: Compassion and Hope*. Ed. Karen Malpede.
       New York: Drama Book, 1983. 173-76. Also contains
       "On Strindberg and Sexism."

B23   "On Summer." *Playbill* 27 June 1960: 25-27.

B24   "Original Prospectus for the John Brown Memorial Theatre of
       Harlem." *Black Scholar* 10 (July/Aug. 1979): 14-15.

B25   "Playwrighting: Creative Constructiveness."   *Annals of Psy-*

chotherapy (Monograph 8, *The Creative Use of the Un-conscious by the Artist and by the Psychotherapist*) 5.1 (1964): 13-17. Address to Eighth Annual Conference of the American Academy of Psychotherapists, 5-6 Oct. 1963.

B26   "Quo Vadis." *Mademoiselle* Jan. 1960: 34.

        Hopes for world peace, guaranteed health care for all, a more radical spirit in Negro leadership, and that "our finest painters and writers will dismiss the vogue of unmodified despair in order to pick up the heritage of a nobler art."

B27   "The Scars of the Ghetto." *Monthly Review* 16.10 (Feb. 1965): 588-91.

        Celebrates the spirit of the oppressed American Negro which has been "imprisoned in the ghetto." Calls for sophisticated new leadership if the race is to emerge out of its desperate situation.

B28   "The Shakespearean Experience." *Show* Feb. 1964: 80+.

        Hansberry says her favorite Shakespeare plays are *Othello*, because "there is a sweetness...that lingers long after the tragedy is gone," and *Hamlet*, because "there remains a depth in the Prince that we all know" that "constantly re-engages as we mature."

B29   "Stanley Gleason and the Lights That Must Not Die." *New York Times* 17 Jan. 1960: 10:11-14.

B30   "Strange Flower." *Liberation* 4 (May 1959): 14-15.

B31   "This Complex of Womanhood." *Ebony* 15 (Aug. 1960): 40.

        Briefly reviews the historical and romantic character of Negro women and calls for them, "as Negroes or women," on "behalf of an ailing world which sorely needs" their defiance, to "never accept the notion of--'our place.'"

B32   "Thoughts on Genet, Mailer and the New Paternalism." *Village Voice* 1 June 1961: 10+.

    Remarks that sitting through a "too long evening of *The Blacks*," one is overwhelmed with Genet's "distrust of us; his refusal to honor our longings for communion." Laments Norman Mailer's "lusty acceptance of the romantic racism" of the play.

B33   "Three Hundred Years Later." *Black Collegian* 14 (March/April 1984): 48.

B34   "To Ghana Off the Top of My Head, March 1957." *Black Collegian* 14 (March/April 1984): 48.

B35   "Village Intellect Revealed" (interview, etc.). *New York Times* 31 Oct. 1964: 2:1+.

    In terms of *The Sign in Sidney Brustein's Window*, recalls that her interest in it shifted over the years she worked on it--that the remark from a friend that inspired the play had long been left behind.

B36   "We Are of the Same Sidewalks...." *Freedomways* 20 (3rd Quarter 1980): 197-99.

IV. INTERVIEWS

Interview with Studs Terkel. Chicago, 2 May 1959. Abridged version of *WMFT Chicago Fine Arts Guide* April 1961: 8-14. See also "Make New Sounds: Studs Terkel Interviews Lorraine Hansberry." *American Theatre* Nov. 1984: 5+.

Interview with Patricia Marks. Unpublished. WNYC, New York City, 30 March 1961.

Interview with Nan Robertson. *New York Times* ("Arts and Leisure" Section) 8 March 1959. (Hansberry reportedly denied some things said in this article. She sent a letter of correction to the *New York Times* which was   never published.)

Interview with E.B. White. "Talk of the Town: Playwright." *New Yorker* 35 (9 May 1959): 33-35.

Interview with Ellen Willis. "We Hitch Our Wagons." *Mademoiselle* Aug. 1960: 135. (Hansberry was one of 20 interviewed by this student.)

V. MEDIA PRODUCTIONS

RECORDINGS

Lorraine Hansberry In Her Own Words. Los Angeles: Pacifica Tape Library, BB4497.01 (part 1, 3 cassettes) and BB5348.02 (part 2, 3 cassettes). A tribute by leading theater artists performing from Hansberry's published and unpublished works. Cast includes Anne Bancroft, Lauren Bacall, Bette Davis, Colleen Dewhurst, Melvyn Douglas, Louis Gossett, Julie Harris, James Earl Jones, Angela Lansbury, Geraldine Page, Sidney Poitier, Cicely Tyson, and Hansberry's own recorded speeches and interviews. Narrated by Ossie Davis and Harold Scott. Script and direction by Robert Nemiroff. Produced by Ted Rubin. Broadcast WBAI-FM, New York, 22 January and 9 February 1967.

Lorraine Hansberry on Her Art and the Black Experience. Her work, philosophy, the theater, the Black experience, and the challenge to the artist in mid-century America. New York: Caedmon Records, TC1352.

Lorraine Hansberry Speaks Out: Art and the Black Revolution. New York: Caedmon Records, TC1352, 1972. Interview by Mike Wallace, excerpts from speeches and interviews. Selected and edited with notes by Robert Nemiroff.

A Raisin in the Sun. New York: Caedmon, TRS355 (3 records),

1972. Cast album. Includes Ossie Davis, Ruby Dee, Claudia McNeil, Diana Sands. Directed by Lloyd Richards.

To Be Young, Gifted and Black. New York: Caedmon, TRS342 (3 records), 1971. Cast album. Includes James Earl Jones, Barbara Baxley, Claudia McNeil. Directed by Gigi Cascio and Robert Nemiroff.

FILMS

The Black Experience in the Creation of Drama. Documentary film. Written and produced by Ralph J. Tangney. Narrated by Lorraine Hansberry and Claudia McNeil. Princeton: Films for the Humanities, FFH-128 (35 min., 16 mm. color), 1976. Available on videocassette. A dramatic blend of materials from Hansberry's life and writings. With Sidney Poitier, Ruby Dee, Diana Sands, and Roy Scheider.

Black Theatre: The Making of a Movement. Insight Media, Video #AQ489, New York, 1978. Video (41 minutes) in which filmmaker Woody King, Jr. profiles drama that grew out of the civil rights movement. Features scenes from *A Raisin in the Sun*. Ossie Davis, Ruby Dee, Lloyd Richards and others discuss the development of African-American theater.

A Raisin in the Sun. Directed by Daniel Petrie. Columbia Pictures (128 minutes, 16 mm.), 1961. Cast includes Louis Gossett, Diana Sands, Sidney Poitier, Claudia McNeil, and Ruby Dee.

A Raisin in the Sun. Directed by Bill Duke, PBS American Playhouse (171 minutes), videocassette release of the 1989 production. Cast includes Danny Glover, Esther Rolle, Starletta DuPois, and Kim Yancy. Restores scenes and dialogue cut from the original stage and film versions.

To Be Young, Gifted and Black. Insight Media, Video #AQ760, New York, 1969. Video (28 minutes) features excerpts from the 1969 Cherry Lane production starring Cicely Tyson, Dolores Sutton, Bruce Hall, and Bernard Ward.

To Be Young, Gifted and Black. Directed by Michael A. Schultz. Produced by Robert M. Fresco. WNET, Educational Broadcasting Corporation, 1972. Distributed by Indiana University AV Center, Bloomington (90 minutes, videocassette), RSC-791. Film based on the book and stageplay. Includes Ruby Dee, Roy Scheider, Blythe Danner, Al Freeman Jr., Barbara Barrie, Claudia McNeil.

VI. UNPUBLISHED MATERIALS

A Raisin in the Sun, early draft and pre-Broadway script.

The Arrival of Mr. Todog, transcript of play satirizing *Waiting for Godot*.

Laughing Boy, a book for a musical based on Oliver LeFarge's novel.

Les Blancs, transcript of early draft.

Letter to the editor of *One*, 18 April 1961. Hansberry comments on reports of a split between gay men and lesbians over propagation of a "Bill of Rights for Homosexuals."

The Marrow of Tradition, an adaptation of Charles Chesnutt's work.

The Masters of the Dew, screenplays based upon Jacques Roumain's Haitian novel, *Gouverneurs de la rosée*. The film was never made.

"Memoirs." About family and childhood.

"The New Paternalists." 1961. Expansion of "Thoughts on

Genet, Mailer and the New Paternalism."

"The Origins of Character."   Draft and notes for address to American Academy of Psychotherapists, 5 Oct. 1963. Abridged version published as "Play-wrighting: Creative Constructiveness."

A play about Achnaton, the Egyptian pharaoh.

"Playwright at Work." Transcript of interview with Frank Perry, PBS, WNET, 21 May 1961.

The Sign in Sidney Brustein's Window, transcripts of early draft and acting version.

"Simone de Beauvoir and *The Second Sex*: An American Commentary," 1957. A critical commentary on a book Hansberry said had changed her life.

Toussaint, transcript and manuscript.

Transcript of interview with Eleanor Fisher for CBS, 7 June 1961.

Transcript of interview with Patricia Marks for Radio Station WNYC, New York, 30 March 1961.

VII. ARCHIVAL SOURCES

Hansberry's literary estate, including the bulk of her manuscripts, unpublished papers, and personal memorabilia are part of the estate of her one-time husband and literary executor, Robert Nemiroff.

Articles from *Freedom*, 1951-55, are housed in the Schomburg Center for Research in Black Culture, New York Public Library.

Secondary Bibliography: Reviews

The following is an annotated, chronologically arranged list of reviews concentrating on Hansberry's career as a dramatist, play by play. It also includes reviews of film productions of *A Raisin in the Sun* and the stage musical *Raisin*. (The theatrical reviews refer to a then currently running production.)

A Raisin in the Sun (the drama)

R1   Burnham, Louis E. "Turkey Talk." *Spectator* 9 March 1959: 12.

Cites *A Raisin in the Sun* as the sort of art that Negro writers should be producing. Quotes Hansberry as calling for a revival of a partisan war against the illusions of our time and culture: "'that art is not, should not and when it's at its best, cannot be social.'"

R2   Aston, Frank. "*Raisin in the Sun* is Moving Tale." *New York World Telegram* 12 March 1959.

The play, "written by a Negro" about Negroes and acted, with one exception, by an "all-Negro company," has no ax to grind. "It is an honest drama, catching up real people." It may "rip you to shreds" and "make you proud of human beings."

R3   Atkinson, Brooks. "*A Raisin in the Sun.*" *New York Times* 12

March 1959.

A Raisin in the Sun is honest. Hansberry has not "tipped her play to prove one thing or another." She "has told the inner as well as the outer truth about a Negro family...." Likens the play to Chekhov's *The Cherry Orchard* because of how character is controlled by environment in a blend of humor and pathos.

R4   Chapman, John. *"A Raisin in the Sun* a Glowingly Lovely and Touching Little Play." *New York Daily News* 12 March 1959.

Hansberry's play is "affectionately human, funny and touching." The actors are a "company" and not just a collection of players.

R5   Coleman, Robert. *"Raisin in the Sun* Superior Play." *Daily Mirror* 12 March 1959.

Hansberry has "etched her characters with understanding and told her story with dramatic impact." She has a "keen sense of humor, an ear for accurate speech and compassion for people." She states important truths "without mounting a soapbox."

R6   Kerr, Walter. *"A Raisin in the Sun."* *New York Herald Tribune* 12 March 1959.

Lloyd Richards has directed Hansberry's play with "a fluid, elusive, quick-tempered grace that permits no moment--and no shade of desperation--to pass unexamined." An "impressive first play, beautifully acted."

R7   McClain, John. *"A Raisin in the Sun* Gives a Wonderful Emotional Evening." *Journal American* 12 March 1959.

The play proved that "when these people [Negroes] create and participate in something for themselves they can make the rest of us look silly." The play is a "stupendous unsegregated hit" in which the "absolute honesty of the speech and behavior of the characters was most impressive." There are no "Uncle Toms" and no "self-conscious intellectuals" here.

R8   Watts, Richard. "Honest Drama of a Negro Family." *New York Post* 12 March 1959.

   A Raisin in the Sun is a "moving and impressive drama" in which Hansberry sets down "without recourse to trickery or sentimentality the stresses and strains that torment a poor Negro family." "Compassionate candor" and "excellent acting" compliment the play.

R9   Tynan, Kenneth. "Review of *A Raisin in the Sun.*" *New Yorker* 21 March 1959: 100-2.

   While the play is not without its sentimentality, the "Negro actors" draw one into the "unresisting world of their making, their suffering, their thinking, and their rejoicing." The play generates the same kind of sympathy as Odets' *Awake and Sing* did twenty-four years before.

R10   Anon. *Time* 22 March 1959: 58+.

   A Raisin in the Sun is a work "of genuine dramatic merit." It "might be somber, or merely sentimental, if its milieu were not so sharply observed, its speech so flavorful, and its infectious sense of fun so caustic."

R11   Anon. "With a Wallop." *Newsweek* 23 March 1959: 76.

   A Raisin in the Sun is one of most "stirring and revealing productions of the year." Hansberry has "walloped home" emotional crises that "repeatedly smash through the barrier between players and playgoers."

R12   Atkinson, Brooks. "*Raisin in the Sun*: Vivid Drama About a Poor Negro Family." *New York Times* 25 March 1959.

   Hansberry has written a "homely play about the day-to-day anxieties of a Negro family...some of the troubles are uproariously funny; some of them are harrowing." The acting is "vehement...but never excessive."

R13   Anon. "*A Raisin in the Sun* Voted Best Play of the Year." *Jet* 26 March 1959: 60-62.

   Hansberry's play received six votes for the Drama Critics Award; Williams' *Sweet Bird of Youth* and MacLeish's *J. B.* received five each.

R14   Clurman, Harold. "Theatre." *Nation* 4 April 1959: 301.
        A Raisin in the Sun is an "authentic," realistic
        play, a portrait of "the aspirations, anxieties, ambitions
        and contradictory pressures affecting humble Negro folk
        in an American big city."

R15   Hewes, Henry. "A Plant Grows in Chicago." *Saturday Review* 4
        April 1959: 28.
        A Raisin in the Sun is a play about "real people"
        who only happen to be "colored people." Their "inner
        family joys and anxieties are universal ones." It is "less
        than a great play," but "better than some this season."

R16   Driver, Tom F. *"A Raisin in the Sun." New Republic* 13 April
        1959: 21.
        As a piece of dramatic writing, *A Raisin in the
        Sun* is "old fashioned." As "something near to the con-
        science of a nation troubled by injustice to Negroes, it is
        emotionally powerful. Much of its success is due to our
        sentimentality over the 'Negro question.'" While the play
        is "moving as a theatrical experience," the emotions it en-
        genders are not relevant to the social and political reali-
        ties.

R17   Hayes, Richard. "The Weathers of the Heart." *Commonweal* 17
        April 1959: 81.
        A Raisin in the Sun's power does not come from
        "intimations and magnitudes of conception," its "style,"
        or newness of vision. Its power comes from "the weath-
        ers of the heart"--the potency of human emotion and
        Hansberry's ability to put it into form. It is the "poetry
        of human concern to which we respond," as is the case
        with our response to Theodore Dreiser's works.

R18   Anon. "On Broadway: *A Raisin in the Sun." Theatre Arts* 43
        (May 1959): 22-23.
        Hansberry's people in *A Raisin in the Sun* have

"the faculty of being readily identifiable types, capable of gaining universal recognition and sympathy." Her actors, except one, are Negro, "and the conviction she [and they] have achieved is something that arises from firsthand knowledge and experience."

R19   Anon. "Playboy After Hours: Theatre." *Playboy* 6 (May 1959): 14+.

Hansberry's *A Raisin in the Sun* is "a smashing show."

R20   Anon. *"Raisin in the Sun." Catholic World* 189 (May 1959): 159.

Hansberry's is an "honest play of contemporary life, splendidly acted," and "deserves a warm welcome."

R21   Anon. *"A Raisin in the Sun." Theatre* 1 (May 1959): 31.

A very positive review of *A Raisin in the Sun*, a play that is "rich in humor, pathos, tears, and laughter, situation, thoughts and resolution."

R22   Lewis, Theophilus. *"Raisin in the Sun." America* 2 May 1959: 286-87.

A Raisin in the Sun is a "study of Negro character under pressure." This character is "sustained by a religious prop and a masochistic sense of humor." It "often bends but barely breaks" because Negroes "have to be tough to survive." Hansberry wisely declines to let her play lapse into "interracial propaganda."

R23   Weales, Gerald. "Thoughts on *A Raisin in the Sun." Commentary* 27 (June 1959): 527-530.

Reviews the climate of Broadway (and in America) for Negro and other ethnic artists. Hansberry, like other Negro playwrights, "must try to write not a Negro play, but a play in which the characters are Negroes." Suggests that Hansberry being "the first Negro woman to have a play on Broadway, had its influence on the voting critics" for the Drama Critics Award.

R24   Anon. "Domestic Drama from the Top Drawer." *Theatre Arts*
        43 (July 1959): 5.
                A positive review of *A Raisin in the Sun* with
        several photographs of the production.

R25   Anon. "London Critics Cool to *Raisin in the Sun.*" *New York*
        Times 5 Aug. 1959: 32:3.
                While the play was "warmly applauded" by the
        audience, most of the critics found its pace too slow.
        Most of them liked the theme and acting.

R26   Brein, Alan. "Suspected Persons." *Spectator* 14 Aug. 1959:
        189.
                While *A Raisin in the Sun* deals with important
        social issues, the "Negroes on stage are stage Ne-
        groes...stock Samuel French types." It is "embarrass-
        ingly overacted" by some of the performers.

R27   Alvarez, A. "That Evening Sun." *New Statesman* 15 Aug. 1959:
        190.
                Although *A Raisin in the Sun* is occasionally
        "trite," it makes for "an extraordinary compelling" eve-
        ning's theater. Hansberry uses powerful rhetoric to ex-
        plore such issues as "natural dignity."

R28   Arnow, Robert. "Juicy Raisin." *Jewish Currents* 18.8 (Sept.
        1959): 38-39.
                Hansberry's characters in *A Raisin in the Sun*
        "grow in stature as they grope their way up their Everest
        of moral predicaments," leaving the audience "with a
        dazzling vision of the modern situation of mankind." The
        play shows the "influence of Sean O'Casey, the play-
        wright of Dublin slum-dwellers," and Hansberry's dia-
        logue and humor are "veritably in the manner of Sholem
        Aleichem."

R29   Lewis, Theophilus. "Social Protest in *A Raisin in the Sun.*"
        Catholic World Oct. 1959: 31-35.
                A Raisin in the Sun is a "first rate drama" that

deserved the Circle Critics Award. There are no Freudian implications. It has no "clinical motivation, no symbolism. It is a straight forward social drama, at least superficially, written in a naturalistic style that is refreshing in its simplicity."

R30   Anon. "*A Raisin in the Sun* Staged in Soviet." *New York Times* 14 Nov. 1961: 47:5.

A Raisin in the Sun was staged "in a plain, realistic manner without stage effects" in the Central Army Theatre in Moscow.

R31   Cain, Scott. "Radiant *Raisin in the Sun* Becomes More Universal." *Atlantic Journal* 21 Sept. 1979.

Because in 1979, when more people than ever "feel they are crushed financially and their prospects are limited," Hansberry's play seems "more universal than it did in the past."

R32   Rich, Frank. "Theater: *Raisin in the Sun* Anniversary in Chicago." *New York Times* 5 Oct. 1983: C24.

This revival production "falls short" of the original, but the play's strengths are still apparent. The production is too conscious of the original, which limits it. It "contains performances that look like dogged, at times strangulated imitations of those by Sidney Poitier, Diana Sands, Ruby Dee."

R33   Johnson, Malcolm. "*Raisin in the Sun* Makes Grand Return to New Haven." *Hartford (Conn.) Courant* 9 Nov. 1983.

Sadly, Hansberry's *A Raisin in the Sun* continues to be relevant because, still, for "most of black America, the dream is still deferred, the chemistry for explosion is still at flashpoint."

R34   Winn, Steven. "A Playwright's Landmark." *San Francisco Examiner* 4 March 1984.

Hansberry's *A Raisin in the Sun* holds "even more meaning in terms of the black movement today than it did nearly 10 years ago....Black militants will never know 'where it's at' until they know 'where it's from.'"

R35   Dodds, Richard. "*Raisin* Glows at Ethiopian Theatre." *Times-Picayune (New Orleans)* 23 April 1984.
       Hansberry's *A Raisin in the Sun* is still relevant because despite "radical changes in matters racial...many of the destructive forces shown working within and without one family as it tries to pull itself out of poverty remain in place today."

R36   Pollack, Joe. "A Magnificent Revival of *A Raisin in the Sun*." *St. Louis Post Dispatch* 10 Sept. 1984.
       Twenty-five years after its premiere, the play is still "wonderful." "It is today's story and today's family--and it will be tomorrow's family, whether black or white or yellow or brown."

R37   Collins, William B. "Local Incidents Make *Raisin* a Timely Revival." *Philadelphia Inquirer* 1 Dec. 1985.
       Notes how current racial hostility between blacks and whites demonstrates the social relevance of *A Raisin in the Sun*. Moreover, director Gregory Poggi asserts that the play is about "human values...about family, and it is very much about black people recognizing their own strengths."

R38   Collins, William B. "Theater: Revival of Hansberry's *Raisin in the Sun*." *Philadelphia Inquirer* 6 Dec. 1985.
       There is "something timeless about [the characters'] assertion of pride, about their dignity and their courage as they set out from Chicago's black ghetto for a place of their own."

R39   Tallmer, Jerry. "*Raisin*: A Play for Today and Tomorrow." *New York Post* 6 Aug. 1986.
       Quotes director Harold Scott as saying "Hansberry's work is timeless in a way I don't feel any other plays of our black literature, that came after, were

as timeless. They're all hate plays--'I hate white'--not plays of love. Anger against something never survives as much as anger *for* something."

R40   Barnes, Clive. *"Raisin* Still Makes You Care." *New York Post* 15 Aug. 1986.
         Hansberry's *A Raisin in the Sun* is not "simply concerned with the integration of housing." The issues of black feminism and nationalism form a "counterpoint" for the drama's action. However many "false notes" Hansberry may sound, the play still "makes you care."

R41   Watt, Douglas. "A Sweetened *Raisin* Revival." *New York Daily News* 15 Aug. 1986.
         A Raisin in the Sun remains "passionate and moving." The revival includes the addition of material omitted from the original staging.

R42   Feldberg, Robert. *"Raisin*: A Poignant Revival." *Hackensack, New Jersey Record* 29 Aug. 1986.
         Despite some "technical awkwardness in arranging scenes and an occasional conversation that drifts into speech-making--understandable flaws in a young writer," Hansberry's *A Raisin in the Sun* is a "total theatrical experience."

R43   Erstein, Hap. "The Sun Doesn't Shine on Revived *Raisin.*" *Washington (D.C.) Times* 17 Nov. 1986.
         Hansberry's play is, finally, dated in this silver anniversary revival of *A Raisin in the Sun*. Perhaps the satire on the play in George C. Wolfe's *The Colored Museum* is apt in its suggestion that Hansberry's characters are now "merely stereotypes of a previous generation's consciousness." Esther Rolle "falls short" of filling the slippers of "rock solid" Grandma Lena.

R44   Anderson, Lucia. *"Raisin* Explodes with Powerful Life." *Potomac News (Virginia)* 18 Nov. 1986.
         This revival, starring Esther Rolle as Lena, is

magnificent. Of interest, too, is the character Beneatha, whose heart is set on becoming a doctor and is trying to "find herself" between "the slavish imitation of whites and total reversion to her African background."

R45   Rousuck, J. Wynn. "This *Raisin* Gets Too Much Respect: Reverential Treatment of Text Lacks Vitality." *Baltimore Sun* 28 April 1988.

Hansberry's "themes of dignity, personal growth, and familial love ring out loud and true," but the production, starring Esther Rolle, treats the text with such reverence, that "some of the liveliness is lost." Despite the length and slow pacing, the "play's greatness comes through."

R46   Ungar, Arthur. *"Raisin in the Sun* Still Relevant: Lorraine Hansberry's 1959 Drama Launches 8th American Playhouse Season." *Christian Science Monitor* 30 Jan. 1989: 11.

Praises PBS's American Playhouse for producing *A Raisin in the Sun.* While the play has much to say about "black family matriarchy, the complex levels of black society, and the struggle of the underclass to clamber out of the ghetto," this "TV version" overstates its case. Includes a brief interview with Robert Nemiroff.

R47   Collins, Monica. "At 30, *Raisin* is Still Plump with Passion." *USA Today* 31 Jan. 1989: 3D.

PBS's production of *A Raisin in the Sun* demonstrates that Hansberry's thirty-year-old play "still has a highly charged currency and relevance." It "strikes with the same deep fury as Arthur Miller's *Death of a Salesman.* Both concern themselves with families in crisis and "bellow out into the universe a lament for the human condition."

R48   Vaughan, Kevin E. "With *Raisin* Revisited, Bias Still Defers Dreams." *Philadelphia (Penn). Inquirer* 4 April 1993.

The brilliance of *A Raisin in the Sun* was Hans-

berry's "ability to vie the circumstances of her characters...through the lens of...sometimes convergent and di-
vergent points of view--religion, law and Afrocentricity--
while honestly portraying the effects of racism on a family whose future we are left to ponder."

A Raisin in the Sun (the film)

R49   Robinson, Louie. "Movie of the Week." *Jet* 9 March 1961.
                Hansberry's stage play "has been transferred to
        the motion picture screen with all of its earthy drama and
        humor intact--a rare feat in movie making." It is worthy
        of an Academy Award.

R50   Knight, Arthur. "Theatre Into Film." *Saturday Review* 25 March
        1961: 34.
                The film transcends the "limitations of its single
        set and its three-act construction." This is achieved by
        "playing each shot for its full dramatic weight and in-
        tensity, and by permitting the camera to probe each scene
        for the utmost revelation of character and milieu."

R51   Tube. "*A Raisin in the Sun*." *Variety* 29 March 1961.
                This is a "stirring film...an important, worth-
        while, timely social document, one that deals with genu-
        ine, everyday people who will be universally understood."

R52   Beckley, Paul V. "*A Raisin in the Sun*." *New York Herald
        Tribune* 30 March 1961.
                The film is "one of the best" of the year--as
        "tight a weave of humor and pathos as you're likely to
        see anywhere."

R53   Crowther, Bosley. "*A Raisin in the Sun*." *New York Times* 30
        March 1961: 24:1.
                While the movie remains "stagelike," Hans-
        berry's fine play "has been turned into an equally fine
        screen drama." Sidney Poitier is "lithe and electric";
        Claudia McNeil is "stolid, voluminous and serene."

R54   Anon. "*A Raisin in the Sun.*" *Time* 31 March 1961.
             The film is a "writhing, vital mess of tenement
       realism." Hansberry apparently felt "obliged to sprinkle
       the mess occasionally with Mammy's own brand of
       brown sugar, [and] to douse it frequently with the skim
       milk of human kindness that too often passes for social
       concern." The film is a "charming, passionate, superior
       soap opera in blackface."

R55   Anon. "*A Raisin in the Sun*: Expect Movie Version to Rival
       Stage Play's Huge Success." *Ebony* 16 (April 1961):
       53-56.
             To add realism to the film, fifteen percent of its
       scenes were shot on location in and around Chicago. In-
       cludes several photographs from the film.

R56   Mekas, Jonas. "Movie Journal." *Village Voice* 6 April 1961.
             The movie *A Raisin in the Sun*, while blown up
       "high" by the critics, really "stinks." It is "actually a
       Hollywoodish attempt at a 'message' film: the race
       problem up North." It says that the "ideal of the Negro is
       to get into one of those suburban houses advertised in the
       Saturday Evening Post, with lawns, good neighbors, and
       rosy kitchens."

R57   Hartung, Philip T. "Angry Young Black Man." *Commonweal* 7
       April 1961: 46.
             As a movie, *A Raisin in the Sun* "is rather
       static...relying greatly on close-ups and dialogue." Yet it
       provides a "compelling and percipient picture of Negro
       life."

R58   Oliver, Edith. "The Sun Still Shines." *New Yorker* 8 April 1961:
       164-65.
             The play *A Raisin in the Sun* has been turned
       into a "pretty good movie." While the excitement is still
       there, "the play's intimacy--its most valuable and perish-
       able quality--has disappeared."

R59   Petrie, Daniel. "Film Review of *A Raisin in the Sun.*" *America* 8
        April 1961: 133.
                The film is a "welcome phenomenon, a powerful
        drama about basically decent, ordinary, likable people."

R60   Anon. "Listen, Don't Look." *Newsweek* 10 April 1961: 103.
                The words are fine in the film, but most of the
        action takes place in one small apartment, not enough to
        make a "real movie." "The play is too much the thing."

R61   Anon. "*A Raisin in the Sun.*" *Life* 21 April 1961: 52D.
                The play's point--"that honor wins over ma-
        terialism"--is "imperfectly presented" in the film. The
        action on the screen seems "too tightly limited to theater
        dimensions."

R62   Anon. "*A Raisin in the Sun.*" *Films in Review* May 1961.
                "The interest which this film engenders derives
        less from the story than from the various attitudes toward
        the Negro problem revealed by the dialogue."

The Sign in Sidney Brustein's Window

R63   Chapman, John. "*Sign in Sid Brustein's Window* Has Much
        Talk and Less Drama." *New York Daily News* 16 Oct.
        1964.
                Unlike *A Raisin in the Sun*, Hansberry's new
        play is "not warm, compact and direct." It is
        "absorbing" here and there, but it is "wordy and played
        scene by scene, not as a theatrical whole." Speculates
        that the failed play is due to Hansberry's having gone
        through psychoanalysis.

R64   Kerr, Walter. "*Sign in Sidney Brustein's Window*--Kerr Reviews
        Hansberry Play." *New York Herald Tribune* 16 Oct.
        1964.
                Getting at the "good things" in Hansberry's play
        "is like trying to decide when to step on an escalator.
        You never know which step to take." Yet there are good

things in the play which is packaged too loosely.

R65   McClain, John. "Drama of Life in the Village Lights Up at
       Times." *Journal American* 16 Oct. 1964.
              Notes that the playbill for *The Sign in Sidney
       Brustein's Window* says that Hansberry's favorite activ-
       ity is "'a great deal of talking.'" Unfortunately, this
       shows up in her play. While a great deal of the talk is
       good, it takes "too long to get it sorted out."

R66   Nadel, Norman. "Brustein is Unfocused; So is Play." *New York
       World Telegram* 16 Oct. 1964.
              Hansberry's concern with "moral values, dedica-
       tion, betrayal, self-deceit, and the fragility of human rela-
       tions" is lost in a play which is "labored and long, insuf-
       ficiently focused, and unable to stir much sympathetic or
       empathic feeling in the audience."

R67   Taubman, Howard. "Lorraine Hansberry's Play at Long-acre."
       New York Times 16 Oct. 1964: 32:1.
              Although there are lines in *The Sign in Sidney
       Brustein's Window* "that shine with humor, tremble with
       feeling and summon up a vision of wisdom and integrity,"
       the play lacks concision and cohesion. Hansberry is also
       "evidently determined to use" the play "to tick off some
       of her pet peeves" like using an effeminate playwright to
       poke fun at the avant-guard style of theater, and making a
       "mordant comment on homosexuality."

R68   Watts, Richard. "Idealist in Greenwich Village." *New York Post*
       16 Oct. 1964.
              The Sign in Sidney Brustein's Window, wherein
       Hansberry explores matters of "moral responsibility,"
       "has some scenes of power and insight, and is written
       with forthright integrity," but it suffers "from overbur-
       dening itself with material for lamentation."

R69   Cooke, Richard P. "Miss Hansberry's Success." *Wall Street
       Journal* 19 Oct. 1964: 20.

> *The Sign in Sidney Brustein's Window* successfully reaches "into the turbulence of contemporary New York life" and comes up "with a true report which is also a work of dramatic art." The play demonstrates that Hansberry is not just a "one shot author," but a creative playwright "who has been adding to her knowledge of human beings."

R70 Anon. "Guilt Collectors." *Time* 23 Oct. 1964: 67.

> *The Sign in Sidney Brustein's Window* has "too many minds of its own. It is overloaded, overwritten and overwrought." The play has "diversity without direction." It "endlessly circles its own conversation pit."

R71 McCarten, John. "Hansberry's Potpourri." *New Yorker* 24 Oct. 1964: 93.

> *The Sign in Sidney Brustein's Window* rings false. Most of the characters, in particular Sidney, "sound off furiously, but...the content of their windy utterances isn't worth all the to-do."

R72 Gilman, Richard. "Borrowed Bitchery." *Newsweek* 26 Oct. 1964: 101-2.

> *The Sign in Sidney Brustein's Window* is a sort of "inverted miracle" in which Hansberry "manages to distort so many things--taste, intelligence, craft--and be simultaneously perverse as a dramatist, social commentator, political oracle, and moral visionary." The drama is a "union of bitchiness with sentimentality" in which Hansberry's "venomous anger" takes the form of hatred of homosexuals, liberals, abstract artists, nonrealistic playwrights, and white people unwilling to commit suicide.

R73 Hewes, Henry. "He Who Laughs First." *Saturday Review* 31 Oct. 1964: 31.

> In *The Sign in Sidney Brustein's Window*, Hansberry presents an assortment of characters, "each of whom comes to terms with his or her capacity to accept

relative values and limited satisfactions." Her "honesty,
her accuracy of observation, and her superior dialogue
triumph to a considerable extent over her failure to fulfill
an ambitious design."

R74   Taubman, Howard. "Allowing For Flaws: Tolerance in Musi-
      cals Greater Than Plays." *New York Times* 1 Nov. 1964:
      1.
              While   Hansberry's   *The   Sign   in   Sidney
      Brustein's Window "reflects passion, intelligence, and a
      point of view" and "knows how to be in earnest without
      pomposity," because of its mixed reviews it will have a
      harder time with the public--unlike musicals (like the
      similarly reviewed *Golden Boy*) for which the public has
      a taste.

R75   Sheed, Wilfred. "The Stage." *Commonweal* 6 Nov. 1964: 197.
              In *The Sign in Sidney Brustein's Window*, "the
      individual segments have been sharpened to a squeaky
      point, but the Grand Design has been lost." "Any one of
      its plots would make a good play, if the other plots would
      leave it alone." Too many potentially powerful scenes
      are "switched off" too quickly in the interest of "pace and
      zest."

R76   Clurman, Harold. *"The Sign in Sidney Brustein's Window."*
      Nation 9 Nov. 1964: 340.
              Hansberry's play tries to say too much, indeed
      "everything." It aims to depict the "morass of our times,"
      the disillusionment of the urban life among the
      "intelligentsia," and then suggests a "cure" through
      "commonsense, kindness, and understanding." Yet noth-
      ing is dramatized. "Self explanation takes the place of
      revelation."   She has Sidney debunk homosexuality,
      "seeing no special grace or sin in it, but only another
      form of pleasure."

R77   Braine, John. "Theatre Uptown." *Village Voice* 26 Nov. 1964:
      17+.

The Sign in Sidney Brustein's Window is a great play. The "drama critics, largely because of the crippling limitations under which they work, haven't recognized the play's greatness." Hansberry "doesn't know how to create a character who is not...gloriously diverse, illuminatingly contradictory, heart-breakingly alive." Claims enthusiastically that the play shows that Hansberry sees homosexuals as people who victimize others, corrupt youth, and feels that homosexuality "isn't another kind of love; it is a betrayal of love."

R78   Ford, Clebert. "Lorraine Hansberry's World." *Liberator* 4 (Dec. 1964): 9.

        The Sign in Sidney Brustein's Window deals with the problems of intellectual honesty. Briefly reviews Hansberry's life of social commitment and artistry.

R79   Neal, Lawrence P. *"The Sign in Sidney Brustein's Window."* *Liberator* 4 (Dec. 1964): 25.

        The Broadway critics "missed the point" on this one. *The Sign in Sidney Brustein's Window* is concerned with the same thing as *A Raisin in the Sun*--"the necessity of making ethical decisions of a fundamental nature, decisions which go to the core of the dilemma facing black people today: what will be the relationships between the black man and the overall...white society and Western civilization?"

R80   Lewis, Theophilus. *"The Sign in Sidney Brustein's Window."* *America* 5 Dec. 1964: 758.

        The Sign in Sidney Brustein's Window proves that Hansberry is not a "one shot" author. She has written a "delectable chiaroscuro of life in the Village."

R81   Anon. *"The Sign in Sidney Brustein's Window."* *National Review* 23 March 1965: 250.

        The Sign in Sidney Brustein's Window should have closed on opening night. Hansberry has "not felt it necessary to do more than lightly rehash the content of the thirties proletarian theatre."

R82   Redding, Saunders. "Book Corner." *Crisis* 73.3 (March 1966):
       175-76.
               The Sign in Sidney Brustein's Window is a good
       play that just misses being great. It deals with a "modern
       man in confrontation with a world he never made and
       which he must remake to conform to the definition of
       himself."

R83   Novick, Julius. "It's Good to Know Who Lorraine Hansberry
       Was." *New York Times* 27 June 1971: 7.
               While *The Sign in Sidney Brustein's Window*
       has its problems, you can "be moved...even by what your
       rationality rejects as melodramatic and implausible...."
       The "explosive sufferings of the characters...and a sense
       of the author's devoted spirit moving with clumsy passion
       behind them" are inspiring.

R84   Barnes, Clive. *"The Sign in Sidney Brustein's Window."* *New
       York Times* 27 Jan. 1972: 44:1.
               A new production of *The Sign in Sidney
       Brustein's Window* with music is "flawed" and at times
       sinks "into melodrama," "but it has the good red blood of
       Broadway success running in it."

R85   Gottfried, Martin. *"The Sign in Sidney Brustein's Window."*
       Women's Wear Daily 27 Jan. 1972.
               The original production was "clumsy" and the
       musical revival is "clumsy." The play is "more con-
       cerned with argument than with a story, its characters are
       stereotypes instead of people and it tries to fix itself by
       addition rather than discipline."

R86   Watt, Douglas. "Fine Evening at Sidney Brustein's." *New York
       Daily News* 27 Jan. 1972.
               While there are so many "funny" and "touching"
       things in the musical revival of the play, "there is a feel-
       ing of cold calculation in the writing." "People say

amusing and cutting things and create a superficial impression of being real persons with real problems, but one just doesn't believe it."

R87   Watts, Richard. *"The Sign in Sidney Brustein's Window."* New York Post 27 Jan. 1972.
       The original play had "excellent material but seemed...too cluttered for its own good." The same may be said for the musical revival, which has added some songs by a quartet "on the sidelines." Yet there is no disputing "the fact that it has a number of admirable scenes and several striking and original characters."

R88   Heldman, Irma Pascal.   "Miss Hansberry's Tender Drama." *Wall Street Journal* 28 Jan. 1972.
       Despite evident flaws, *The Sign in Sidney Brustein's Window* "is a wise, tender, tasteful portrait of humanity that is also very funny." The production includes a quartet "that is intended to provide transition via song--a sort of updated Greek chorus. It is entirely superfluous."

R89   Thurston, Chuck. "There's a Message Here, in All the Talk." *Detroit Free Press* 28 April 1976.
       The Sign in Sidney Brustein's Window, set in 1964, has "a lot to say about prejudices, reform movements, Walden Pondism and student rebellion." "Old message pieces, like old hometowns, should be revisited only out of curiosity." The play needs "severe trimming to suit today's mood."

R90   Nelson, Don. *"Sign* Still Illumines Life." *New York Daily News* 9 Feb. 1980.
       In her "drama [*The Sign in Sidney Brustein's Window*] of belief and responsibility," Hansberry "orchestrates our emotions, directing our anger here, our tenderness there, so that during the process we see some of us in all the characters."

R91   Jacobs, Tom. "Actors Alley Stages Little-Known Work from *Raisin* Playwright." *Los Angeles Daily News* 11 July 1991.

> *The Sign in Sidney Brustein's Window* is an uneven work which presents "a rather bleak choice between soulless nihilism or naive idealism, ultimately suggesting we must keep fighting the good fight, in spite of the many risks that entails."

To Be Young, Gifted and Black

R92   Duberman, Martin. "Theatre 69: Black Theater." *Partisan Review* 36 (1969): 490.

> In *To Be Young, Gifted and Black*, some of Hansberry's "attitudes (though not all) are decidedly out of fashion with black playwrights now." The self-portrait she draws of herself as a young co-ed resembles a heroine in any standard *McCall's* serial.

R93   Shepard, Richard F. "Theater: Hansberry Life." *New York Times* 3 Jan. 1969: 15.

> *To Be Young, Gifted and Black* is a "moving evening, sentimental in the best sense of the word." It "takes no time to mourn and plenty of time to laugh, muse and occasionally burst into a salvo of rage at the way things are, when they should be somehow different."

R94   Oliver, Edith. "Off Broadway." *New Yorker* 11 Jan. 1969: 58.

> *To Be Young, Gifted and Black* is not so successful because the performance as a whole is "not quite good," and because "excerpts from letters and journals are better read privately than heard."

R95   Silber, Irwin. "Black Is the Color." *Guardian* 25 Jan. 1969: 19.

> *To Be Young, Gifted and Black* is not a sentimental play of memories; it is "an intensely theatrical and emotionally stirring event."

R96   Clurman, Harold. "Theatre." *Nation* 28 April 1969: 548.

To Be Young, Gifted and Black, like Hansberry's other work, shows her outstanding qualities: "sweetness and balance, a healthy intelligence, a secure spirit. She is perceptive, dignified, clear." Her statements are "not soft; they are firmly planted."

R97   Hentoff, Nat. *"To Be Young, Gifted and Black." New York Times* 25 May 1969: 11:1:5.

To Be Young, Gifted and Black is a "whirl of proving, celebrating, hoping, laughing, despairing, and moving on." It is not an "encapsulation of the 'We Shall Overcome' time of recent...history." Includes comment on Hansberry's vision and social concerns as they are manifested in her plays.

R98   Weales, Gerald. *"To Be Young, Gifted and Black." Commonweal* 5 Sept. 1969: 542-43.

To Be Young, Gifted and Black is a "disgraceful presentation." The play "made a mockery of Miss Hansberry's talents, destroyed everything that is good and subtle in her work." "If Nemiroff's mosaic were to be taken at face value, it would be necessary to assume that Miss Hansberry was a gushy little girl," while her published plays show her as an artist of "wit and intelligence" with a "strong sense of social and political possibility...."

R99   Barnes, Clive. "Black Theater: Of Politics and Passion." *New York Times* 22 Sept. 1969: 36.

To Be Young, Gifted and Black is a fascinating adaptation. It is interesting because it shows Hansberry to be "far more militant in her letters than in her plays." She was "clearly, and understandably, more radical as a person than as a playwright."

R100   Carroll, Carroll. *"Young, Gifted* Contains the Beautiful Writing of Lorraine Hansberry." *Variety* 14 Jan. 1970: 84.

Applauds the sensitivity of *To Be Young, Gifted and Black*.

R101   Cyclops. "From a Time of Racial Hope." *Life* 14 Jan. 1972: 14.
               Praises Hansberry's work, most recently the
       television version of *To Be Young, Gifted and Black*. A
       "sensibility manifests itself, particularly when Ruby Dee
       is in charge, that instructs and ennobles." Mentions that
       The Sign in Sidney Brustein's Window is scheduled to
       reopen with an original musical score.

R102   O'Connor, John J. "TV: World of Lorraine Hansberry." *New
       York Times* 20 Jan. 1972: 87.
               "To put it briefly, the 90-minute TV version [of
       To Be Young, Gifted and Black] is superb, in many ways
       better than the outstanding stage production."

R103   Nichols, George E. "Guild's *Young Gifted, Black*." *Hartford
       (Conn.) Courant* 22 May 1976.
               While those portions of *To Be Young, Gifted and
       Black* from Hansberry's plays are "satisfying," in terms
       of one's expectations of theater, "it is a relatively static
       piece" because of the lack of tension arising from the
       parts fashioned from her other writings.

R104   Steele, Mike. "Mixed Blood Theater Opens with *To Be Young,
       Gifted and Black*." *Minneapolis Tribune* 9 July 1977.
               While *To Be Young, Gifted and Black* is not "a
       particularly strong work, tending towards the eulogistic
       rather than the insightful and filled with less than apt se-
       lections from the plays," it has some "very powerful and
       very beautiful moments."

R105   Shorey, Kenneth. "*Gifted and Black* Has Attractive Cast."
       Birmingham (Ala.) News 19 Feb. 1982.
               To Be Young, Gifted and Black is a study in
       "black definitions and the search for meaning, 'the why
       and the how of life,'" as well as a chronicle of Hans-
       berry's "mild flirtations with revolutionary, even Com-
       munist, ideas."

R106   Keating, Douglas J. "Theatre: *To Be Young, Gifted and Black*."

Philadelphia Inquirer 29 June 1985.

Considering the play was "compiled by Hansberry's husband, it is surprisingly unsentimental and rather impersonal." Nemiroff "deliberately plays down" Hansberry's death and creates two characters--Lorraine Hansberry and the Playwright--leaving "it to the theatergoer to synthesize them into one person."

R107   Mazur, Carole. "Get Through Life with Art." *Albuquerque Journal* 6 Feb. 1987.

This production of *To Be Young, Gifted and Black* demonstrates that "family relationships" are among its major themes. Current social realities that have led to the "disruption of the extended [black] family" make this play appropriate for the celebration of Black History Month.

R108   McCulloh, T. H. "Strong But Stark *Gifted* Wraps Up." *Los Angeles Times* 3 April 1996: F3.

To Be Young, Gifted and Black captures the "spirit and essence of Hansberry's personality and the urgent, vital tone of her writing."

Les Blancs

R109   Kroll, Jack. "Between Two Worlds." *Newsweek* 30 Nov. 1970: 98.

Les Blancs is a "metaphor of Miss Hansberry's own difficult position as a black writer caught between the humanism that was natural to her and the violent militancy that she saw as inevitable and even right for black people." Most of the play is simply a debate "between her own unreconciled selves."

R110   Barnes, Clive. "Review of *Les Blancs*." *New York Times* 16 Nov. 1970: 48.

Les Blancs is shallow; "the arguments have all been heard before, and are presented in a very simplistic fashion. Too much of it sounds like political propaganda rather than political debate, and the people in the play are debased to labeled puppets mouthing thoughts, hopes and fears that lace the surprise and vitality of life."

R111   Sainer, Arthur. "Is Terror the Way?" *Village Voice* 19 Nov. 1970: 58.

Despite a Hollywood-like production of *Les Blancs*, Hansberry's intelligence and passion shines through. The play is "a harrowing revelation of what we have brought each other to. A time without answers because the questions have become too urgent."

R112   Gill, Brendan. "The Theatre: Things Go Wrong." *New Yorker* 21 Nov. 1970: 104.

The "splendid performance by James Earl Jones," is a redeeming feature in *Les Blancs*, a play with a "doggedly didactic tone," in which the audience is "lectured to and made to see things in the light that Teacher wishes us to see them and not otherwise."

R113   Kerr, Walter. "Vivid, Stinging, Alive." *New York Times* 29 Nov. 1970: 2:3.

Les Blancs is a "mature work," ready to stand without apology alongside the completed work of our best craftsmen. The gaps in the unfinished play are compensated for "by the candor and drive of the play's speech, speech that might have been mere rhetoric but instead achieves a stage quickness."

R114   Riley, Clayton. "A Black Critic on *Les Blancs*: An Incredibly Moving Experience." *New York Times* 29 Nov. 1970: 3+.

Les Blancs may not be a "great piece of theater," but it is an "incredibly moving experience." The play explores contemporary reality: "ugliness recognized, filth and perversity definitely perceived, in that social order most people will recognize under its formal title--Western Civilization."

R115   Clurman, Harold. *"Les Blancs." Nation* 30 Nov. 1970: 572-73.

"*Les Blancs* is not propaganda, as has been inferred; it is a forceful and intelligent statement of the tragic impasse of white and black relations all over the world." The play transcends the "banalities" of intellectual disputes racial conflicts; "it clarifies, but does not seek to resolve, the historical and human problems involved."

R116   Riley, Clayton. "Theatre Review." *Liberator* Dec. 1970: 19+.

While *Les Blancs* has some flaws "compounded by the obvious demands of the Broadway marketplace," it is a play worth seeing for its insight into the black experience.   It will best be "understood by black people...because it is addressed to them...almost in its entirety, and certainly in spirit."

R117   Clurman, Harold. "Theatre." *Nation* 7 Dec. 1970: 605-6.

Les Blancs is not propaganda on behalf of blacks opposed to whites.   It is a "dramatic statement of the tragedy in human history."   Hansberry was no "'black panther,' but an intelligent, compassionate human being with a gift for lucid dramatic writing...."

R118   Rudin, Seymour. "Theatre Chronicle: Fall 1970." *Massachusetts Review* 12 (Winter 1971):   150-61.

Les Blancs revealed "in its stretchiness, its awkwardness, its sometimes trenchant but too often cliche-ridden dialogue" that Hansberry had not thought through or worked over her material sufficiently "to make the play transcend its now dated, familiar vision of the inevitability of black-white conflict."

R119   Shappes, Morris U. "Diary." *Jewish Currents* 25.1 (Jan. 1971): 22.

Les Blancs, Hansberry's commentary on Genet's *The Blacks*, is a memorable and illuminating experience. The play is anti-white colonialists, but not anti-white.

R120   Weales, Gerald. *"Les Blancs."* *Commonweal* 22 Jan. 1971:
       397.
               What is interesting in *Les Blancs* is "the central
       character, the African who, having learned irony in his
       travels, is balanced between exile and commitment, al-
       ways the observer, until events force him to act...." It
       should be more correctly called a play by Robert Ne-
       miroff and Charlotte Zaltzberg based on an unfinished
       script by Hansberry.

R121   Kraus, Ted M.   "Theatre East."   *Players* 46.3 (Feb.-March
       1971).
               Les Blancs was "a serious play that promised to
       be both powerful and meaningful, but it never progressed
       beyond its primary stating of universal racial conflicts."
       In spite of a strong cast, it "never moved beyond repeat-
       ing its rather obvious philosophical confusions."

R122   Anon.   "Playboy After Hours: Theater."   *Playboy* 18 (April
       1971): 37.
               Notes in passing that a number of white critics
       "generally   sympathetic   to   black-theater   aims
       were...appalled by Miss Hansberry's *Les Blancs*... which
       advocated genocide of nonblacks as a solution to the race
       problem." Black critics countered that "their works are
       intended for black audiences and that white critics are not
       qualified to evaluate them."

R123   Gant, Liz. *"Les Blancs."* *Black World* 20.6 (April 1971): 46-47.
               Les Blancs, a play that shows Hansberry's "Pan
       Africanistic" growth before her death, "should have been
       a glowing tribute to her strong Black mind," but unfortu-
       nately, "has been made victim of a rip-off on the Broad-
       way scene."

R124   Taylor, Robert. *"Les Blancs* Presented by Ensemble Theater."
       Oakland Tribune 12 Nov. 1979.
               "*Les Blancs* remains an unfocused drama, run-
       ning nearly three hours, with a series of political and ra-

cial arguments but few surprises except the final gun-shots."

R125 Winn, Steven. "Gripping Choices in Hansberry's Last Play." *San Francisco Chronicle* 11 June 1986.

    Les Blancs has "compelling" speeches and dramatic encounters, and its "suggestions about a country's struggle for political self-determination are complex and unsettling." The play demonstrates how Hansberry "refused to settle for simple answers or pat dramatic resolutions."

R126 Erstein, Hap. "*Les Blancs* at Arena: Perceptive Black Drama." *Washington (D.C.) Times* 12 Feb. 1988.

    Certainly one of Hansberry's messages "is that talk--an open dialogue between the races--is an important deterrent to bloodshed." But while George Bernard Shaw's theatrical debates are "civilized" and "cool," Hansberry "is too fervent for such gentility." This production "delivers the heat."

R127 Fuchs, Elinor. "Rethinking Lorraine Hansberry." *Village Voice* 15 March 1988: 93+.

    Praises Hansberry's *Les Blancs* as a work which shows that the playwright was not a mere "assimilationist retreading the bourgeois family drama (remember the wicked parody in George Wolfe's *The Colored Museum*)." The play shows her "brilliant geopolitical intelligence, a powerful moral imagination, and an emerging command of the great traditions of Western theater."

R128 Fanger, Iris. "*Les Blancs* Keeps Alive Black Feminist Spirit." *Boston Herald* 8 Jan. 1989.

    For Hansberry, the "spirit of Africa was a female warrior pulling her spear from the earth" as King Arthur took his sword from the stone. The difference was that "Arthur's people had not been the victims of...three centuries of oppression."

R129   Devine, Lawrence. "Detroit Repertory Theatre Bares Souls in *Les Blancs*." *Detroit Free Press* 14 Jan. 1989.

Hansberry, never one "to avoid emotion in her work," is clearly "on the side of African self-determination, but she is wholly aware of its cost." The play "does not defy good acting, it encourages it."

R130   Hayman, Edward. "Words in a World of Revolution: Eloquent Writing Keeps 23-Year-Old African Play Alive." *Detroit News* 17 Jan. 1989.

Les Blancs is driven by the "fury of black nationalism." It is "operatic in scope and structure, full of symbolism and ringing declarations of truth that function as spoken arias." Hansberry's characters, finally neither black nor white, are seeing a "long-standing social system...built on the oppressive but well-intended notion of White Man's Burden--crumble around them."

R131   Friedman, Arthur. "Fine Acting Saves Contrived *Les Blancs*." *Boston Herald* 20 Jan. 1989.

So swept up is Hansberry by her anger that "she sometimes loses her artistic balance." The "raw, discursive play often sinks into polemics; too many set debates slow down its impetus; and Hansberry deals her theme from a lopsided deck."

What Use Are Flowers

R132   Hulbert, Dan. "*Flowers* Shows Spiritual Side of Hansberry." *Atlanta Constitution* 29 July 1994: P25.

A preview of the world premiere of *What Use Are Flowers* at the 14th Street Playhouse. It is a "fable set after a cataclysmic war, about an old hermit trying to instill in 10 orphaned children--who are reverting to savagery--the civilization they can't remember." The playwright reveals her "almost mystical belief in the human spirit."

Raisin (the musical stage play)

R133   Barnes, Clive. *"Raisin." New York Times* 31 May 1973: 49:1.
        This Washington D.C. production of the musical, opening on "Lorraine Hansberry Day," is a "warm and loving work" deserving of the standing ovation it received.

R134   Barnes, Clive. *"Raisin." New York Times* 19 Oct. 1973.
        The musical is strange but good. The present book by Robert Nemiroff and Charlotte Zaltzberg "is perhaps even better than the play. It retains all of Miss Hansberry's finest dramatic encounters," with cutting, honest dialogue. "But the shaping of the piece is slightly firmer and better."

R135   Gottfried, Martin. *"Raisin." Women's Wear Daily* 19 Oct. 1973.
        Raisin is a "skimpily musicalized" version of Hansberry's original drama. The idea of making a musical of the play was a "poor one to begin with," for a musical can not be made of a work that is "not essentially musical."

R136   Watt, Douglas. *"Raisin, a Black Period Musical, Brings Back Raisin in the Sun." New York Daily News* 19 Oct. 1973.
        Raisin is an "efficient, likable and rather bland musical" that "always seems on the verge of striking home but never does." The "poignance" and "urgency" of the original play are "dissipated."

R137   Watts, Richard. "Black Family in Chicago." *New York Post* 19 Oct. 1973.
        There's a lot "of good, solid entertainment" in the musical *Raisin*. It is a "superior work" that follows Hansberry's original drama with "fidelity and respect."

R138   Wilson, Edwin. "Putting Miss Hansberry's Play to Music." *Wall Street Journal* 22 Oct. 1973.

While the musical *Raisin* is not a "landmark" like the play upon which it is based, it is a "strong, stimulating piece of work." While its score "lacks dimension," the rest of the work is impressive enough to make it a hit.

R139   Kerr, Walter. *"Raisin* is Sweet, Could Be Sweeter." *New York Times* 28 Oct. 1973: 11:3:1.

The strength of the musical *Raisin* is the "restless invention" of its "musical underscoring" that spills the action from the four walls of Hansberry's original play "onto the streets" where it blends with realistic speech. Its weakness lies "in the ultimate monotony of its melodic line, sometimes making you wish that a song were over so that the family infighting could get going again."

R140   Kalem, T. E. "The Faith That Faded." *Time* 29 Oct. 1973.

Years after the debut of *A Raisin in the Sun*, blacks are now concerned with such goals as separatism; the hopes of a colorblind society dramatized in the play seem "hopelessly dated." The musical version of the play shoves it further into the "realm of soap operetta." The dances "have the cumulative frenzy of a Holy Roller meeting," but nothing can animate the drama's "faded, though once fashionable faith in integration."

R141   Kroll, Jack. "Angry Dreams." *Newsweek* 29 Oct. 1973.

Hansberry's original play, *A Raisin in the Sun* (by her own admission, a "soap opera") was written to "hit audiences right where they lived." The new musical version relies on the play's "strategy of emotional encirclement," but has lost the "rough underside of the play, its secret anger at the forms black dreams must take in a society both oppressive and spiritually meager."

R142   Clurman, Harold. "Theatre." *The Nation* 12 Nov. 1973: 508.

The musical *Raisin* is certainly not better than the original *A Raisin in the Sun*, and to suggest such is an "insult" to Hansberry. The original play's simple power has been dissipated. Yet it is a better, "juicier," musical than most.

R143 Yvonne. "*Raisin*: Sans Sans D'etre." *Ms*. Dec. 1973: 40.

Regrets that the original drama of moral conflict has been "rearranged," and thus "vulgarized," into a Broadway musical, and that Hansberry's artistic vision has been "edited" by Nemiroff. The musical is a "weak revival supported primarily by Hansberry's established fame."

R144 Greer, Edward G. "Broadway--On and Off." *Drama* 112 (Spring 1974): 60-61.

Because of its "abbreviation to accommodate musical numbers," the musical *Raisin* lacks "Hansberry's original poetry and sensitivity." The musical version is a "mere synopsis [of *A Raisin in the Sun*] with mediocre songs by Judd Woldin and lyrics by Robert Brittan, but with fine dances by its choreographer/director, Donald McKayle."

R145 Anon. "Playboy After Hours: Theater." *Playboy* 21 (Feb. 1974): 38.

The musical *Raisin* is a strong, professional production, the result of Hansberry's husband and literary executor, Robert Nemiroff, "who has been mining her creations with sometimes questionable compulsiveness."

R146 Anon. "Lorraine Hansberry's Play Returns as a Smash Musical." *Sepia* 23.4 (April 1974): 32-37.

A rave review of *Raisin* and how it grew out of Hansberry's "historic" work, *A Raisin in the Sun*. Includes photographs of the musical production.

R147 Jones, Clarence B. "*Raisin, The River Niger* and Theatrical History!" *New York Amsterdam News* 27 April 1974: A2.

Celebrates the fact that *Raisin* deservedly won the "Tony" award for best musical of 1974.

R148   Anon.   "Lorraine Hansberry's Play Becomes Musical Hit."
           Ebony 29.7 (May 1974): 74-80.
                   Notes that much of the forcefulness of the drama
           "seems to get lost or diluted in its musical version," with
           many "black observers" regarding this loss as a fatal flaw
           in *Raisin*. Includes photographs of the production.

R149   Thom, Rose Anne. "The Gypsy Camp." *Dance Magazine* 49
           (April 1975): 89-91.
                   A complimentary review of the technical aspects
           of the musical *Raisin*, including comment on the set de-
           sign, choreography, and musical numbers.

R150   Griffin, Christopher. "Poor Production Sours Spirited *Raisin*."
           Columbus (Ohio) Dispatch 27 March 1984.
                   This is a weak production of the musical *Raisin*,
           a play that is "by no means a dreary treatise on the plight
           of blacks in a racist society." Rather, Hansberry's musi-
           cal "approaches the subject with a healthy helping of hu-
           mor, compassion...and inspired songs."

Secondary Bibliography: Books, Articles, Sections

The following is an annotated, chronologically arranged list of books, articles, and sections concentrating on Hansberry's career as a dramatist. (A list of doctoral dissertations concerning the playwright is included at the end.)

1959-1969

S1   Anon. "The Talk of the Town." *New Yorker* 9 May 1959: 33-35.

   An article quoting Hansberry extensively in which she traces some events in her life and their effects on her as an artist.

S2   Isaacs, Harold R. "Five Writers and Their African Ancestors: Part II." *Phylon* 21.4 (1960): 317-36.

   A Raisin in the Sun is important in its expression of Hansberry's anti-assimilasionist viewpoint and as a dramatization of her Negro nationalism, something most critics of the play missed. Discusses Hansberry's growth as a writer concerned with African-American consciousness, often quoting her directly.

S3   Funke, Lewis. "*A Raisin in the Sun* Nearing First Birthday--Its Author at Work." *New York Times* 6 March 1960.

   Among other things, Hansberry says she is

working on a play about Toussaint L'Ouverture.

S4   Brown, Deming. *Soviet Attitudes Toward American Writing.*
       Princeton: Princeton UP, 1962. 189.
              Notes in passing that, in 1960, along with several
       of Arthur Miller's plays, Hansberry's *A Raisin in the Sun*
       was added to the "Soviet repertoire" alongside such
       drama as Lawrence and Lee's *Inherit the Wind,* Nash's
       The Rainmaker, Saroyan's *The Time of Your Life,* and
       Odets' *The Big Knife.*

S5   Isaacs, Harold R. *The New World of Negro Americans.* New
       York: John Day, 1963. 277-87.
              Focuses on *A Raisin in the Sun*'s sub-theme of
       Africa, and how audiences responded to it. The "new
       shape of the African idea in the American Negro universe
       made its first appearance" in Hansberry's play.

S6   Robinson, Layhmond. "Robert Kennedy Consults Negroes Here
       About North." *New York Times* 25 May 1963: 1+.
              News account of Hansberry and other blacks'
       meeting with Attorney General Kennedy to discuss civil
       rights issues.

S7   Fisher, Diane. "Birthweight Low, Jobs Few, Death Comes
       Early." *Village Voice* 8.33 (6 June 1963): 3+.
              Recounts Hansberry's reaction to and obser-
       vations concerning her (and several other blacks') meet-
       ing with Attorney General Robert Kennedy to discuss
       civil rights issues. "'I don't know why it should matter,'"
       said Hansberry of the disappointing meeting, "'but it
       bothered me that he wouldn't meet my eyes.'"

S8   Anon. "Intellectuals Just Can't Reach Robert Kennedy: The
       Little Man Just Wasn't There." *National Guardian* 13
       June 1963.
              Of the meeting with Attorney General Robert
       Kennedy concerning civil rights, Hansberry is quoted as
       saying, "'What we wanted...was to make clear that we

were not asking for gestures; we were not asking for some window-dressing. He wanted a whole bunch of fancy Negroes to tell him he was great and the Administration was doing a fine job.'"

S9   Davis, Ossie. "The Significance of Lorraine Hansberry." *Freedomways* 5.3 (1965): 397-402.

Asserts that, in spite of the success of *A Raisin in the Sun* and the positive impression it seems to have left on audiences, Hansberry "knew that the American dream held by Mama is as unworkable in this day and age as that held by Walter." The playwright saw that Mama's old-fashioned morality "was no solution to being poor and being black in America, even in the suburbs." It's all in the play, but "we are too busy smiling up at Mama, loving her, blessing her, needing her--to see it." In *The Sign in Sidney Brustein's Window*, however, Hansberry made this dark message crystal clear.

S10   Banta, Lucille. "Lorraine Hansberry." *American Dialog* 2.2 (May/June 1965): 25-27.

Claims Hansberry's philosophy was to "sing America." She "envisioned a day when the word, Negro, would not be followed by the epithet 'problem.'"

S11   France, Arthur. *"A Raisin* Revisited: A Re-evaluation of *A Raisin in the Sun* as a Tragedy." *Freedomways* 5.3 (Summer 1965): 403-10.

Argues that the play is a "tragedy" in the sense that a "tragic hero is one who realizes the inevitability of his doom but persists in the exercise of his will...." To "'have undergone tragedy, to have been destroyed, and yet to live on...'" is an apt description of Walter who, like Antigone, is concerned with how to stay alive and still have a degree of dignity.

S12   Turpin, Waters E. "The Contemporary American Negro Playwright." *CLA Journal* 9 (Sept. 1965): 12-23.

Despite the fact that some may find *A Raisin in*

the Sun to be a soap opera, Hansberry was able to "capture the mood of a time and a group, giving all dramatically symbolic structuring which proved effective theatre." She did well "utilizing the universal group survival motif" in the play.

S13   Laufe, Abe. *Anatomy of a Hit: Long-Run Plays on Broadway from 1900 to the Present Day.* New York: Hawthorn Books, 1966. 297-302.

Discusses why *A Raisin in the Sun* was a Broadway success.

S14   Nemiroff, Robert. "The One Hundred and One 'Final' Performances of *Sidney Brustein*: Portrait of a Play and its Author." *A Raisin in the Sun* and *The Sign in Sidney Brustein's Window.* New York: New American Library, 1966. (Also in expanded twenty-fifth anniversary edition, 1987.)

Recounts the heroic efforts to keep the Broadway production of *The Sign in Sidney Brustein's Window* open after it received considerable negative critical response. Discusses Hansberry's view and characterization of the modern intellectual.

S15   Killens, John Oliver. "Broadway in Black and White." *African Forum* 1.3 (Winter 1966): 66-76.

Mentions that *The Sign in Sidney Brustein's Window* is a "brilliant piece of writing" that was angry and humorous as it dissected "the Great American Myth." Hansberry was suggesting that the white world into which the Youngers wanted to move in *A Raisin in the Sun* was hardly worth their efforts.

S16   Atkinson, Brooks. "Of Plays and Novels." *Saturday Review* 31 Dec. 1966: 26-27.

Praises Hansberry's work and laments that serious plays like *The Sign in Sidney Brustein's Window* have such a hard time of it on Broadway when so many imperfect, "overblown little comedies" and musicals seem to run forever.

S17   Mitchell, Loften. *Black Drama: The Story of the American Negro in the Theatre.* New York: Hawthorn Books, 1967. 180-204.
       Discusses Hansberry's career, noting the praise and criticism she received, including complaints from the black intelligentsia who claimed *A Raisin in the Sun* was really a "white" play espousing white values. Comments on *The Sign in Sidney Brustein's Window,* as well.

S18   Turner, Darwin T. "Negro Playwrights and the Urban Negro." *CLA Journal* 12 (Sept. 1968): 19-25.
       Cites *A Raisin in the Sun* as a play that addresses the realities of blacks living in urban areas.

S19   Abramson, Doris E. *Negro Playwrights in the American Theatre: 1925-1959.* New York: Columbia UP, 1969.
       Reviews Hansberry's life and how her experiences evolved into *A Raisin in the Sun* and *The Sign in Sidney Brustein's Window.* Discusses the themes of the plays and, briefly, some of the critical response to them.

S20   Lewis, Emory. *Stages: The Fifty-Year Childhood of the American Theatre.* Englewood Cliffs: Prentice-Hall, 1969. 155-57.
       Hansberry's *A Raisin in the Sun* showed no "Porgys and Besses rolling their eyes in green pastures" but "honestly etched black people." *The Sign in Sidney Brustein's Window,* in spite of its flaws and a "fumbling" production, showed the playwright's "catholic range of vision."

S21   Miller, Jordan Y. "Lorraine Hansberry." *The Black American Writer Volume II: Poetry and Drama.* Ed. C.W.E. Bigsby. Deland, FL: Everett/Edwards, 1969. 157-70.
       Notes that while today, in light of contemporary racial concerns and events, Hansberry's plays might seem to be somewhat void of "blackness," *A Raisin in the Sun*

is remarkable in that it presents "one of the most volatile of our society's problems, telling it precisely 'like it is,' within the most conventional of dramatic frameworks, without rancor and without violence." It is a problem play about blackness in a white society. *The Sign in Sidney Brustein's Window* is termed a "comedy of sensibility," a fundamentally comic play with serious overtones.

S22   Baldwin, James. "Sweet Lorraine." *Esquire* Nov. 1969: 139-41.

A loving reminiscence about Hansberry and her art. Asserts that in *A Raisin in the Sun*, black audiences recognized the house the Youngers wanted and all the people in it. Black viewers "supplied the play with an interpretative element which could not be present in the minds of white people" which involved a "claustrophobic terror created by their knowledge of the house" as well as "their knowledge of the street." Some of Hansberry's "notes" appear at the conclusion of the article.

S23   Keller, Joseph. "Black Writing and the White Critic." *Negro American Literature Forum* 3 (Winter 1969): 103-10.

The black image is a positive one "only in the works of the 50's and 60's now called 'Negro' by many black critics: *A Raisin in the Sun*, for example." The change in core words from the first part of the play "to its hopeful ending suggests a positive change in self-image." Recent critics find that this "positive change in the family is in the wrong direction."

1970-1979

S24   Riach, W.A.D. "'Telling It Like It Is': An Examination of Black Theatre As Rhetoric." *Quarterly Journal of Speech* 46 (April 1970): 179-86.

Claims that plays speak the language of the audiences they address. In this regard, *A Raisin in the Sun*, unlike some other black works, is "white man's language." "'The radical values that make up Lorraine

Hansberry's fictive worlds...make sense only if projected
to a white or white-seeking audience....'"

S25   Lester, Julius. *"Young, Gifted and Black*: The Politics of Car-
        ing." *Village Voice* 28 (May 1970): 14+.
            Reviews Hansberry's plays, asserting that *To Be
        Young, Gifted and Black* has rightfully brought new at-
        tention to her works. Notes that while Hansberry was
        angry, she was nonetheless "a black artist who lived be-
        yond anger." Rather than anger, "compassion," which
        "can slap a face as easily as it can kiss a cheek, which
        can curse as easily as it can tease," defined her art.

S26   Adams, George R. "Black Militant Drama." *American Imago*
        28 (1971): 107-28.
            Points out that the "correct societal-familial
        value-system, a value-system passed down from Big
        Walter through Lena...is White." "It is clear that what
        occurs on the conscious, social level (Walter's becoming
        mature, responsible, and normal)" is his adoption of this
        value-system. Ironically, Walter and the family's dream
        is "not deferred" indefinitely, as the epigraph to the play
        might suggest. The Youngers are not going "to explode"
        and rebel against "oppressive white power." Thus the ti-
        tle of the play is "puzzling."

S27   Ness, David E. *"The Sign in Sidney Brustein's Window*: A
        Black Playwright Looks at White America." *Freedom-
        ways* 11.4 (1971): 359-66.
            The purpose of the play, as Hansberry herself
        said of the challenge to the dramatist, is "'to find some
        way to show and to encourage the white liberal to stop
        being a liberal and become an American radical.'" The
        drama is concerned "with the question of what it takes to
        change...an ordinary, relatively comfortable, educated
        middle-class Jewish liberal into a radical."

S28   Yarbrough, Camille. "'Today I Feel Like Somebody.'" *New
        York Times* 18 April 1971: 3.

The actress in *To Be Young, Gifted and Black* speaks of the rich experiences she and black audiences have in the mutual experience of the play.

S29   Holtan, Orley I. "Sidney Brustein and the Plight of the American Intellectual." *Players* 46.5 (June/July 1971): 222-25.
        The Sign in Sidney Brustein's Window is about how Sidney, the intellectual, must come to see the world with "open-eyed commitment." The themes of the play relate "to the plight of the intellectual in a corrupt society, in which nonetheless he must live and from which he cannot flee."

S30   Hays, Peter L. "*Raisin in the Sun* and *Juno and the Paycock*." *Phylon* 33.2 (Summer 1972): 175-76.
        Notes the parallel to and influences of Sean O'Casey's play on Hansberry.

S31   Farrison, Edward W. "Lorraine Hansberry's Last Dramas." *CLA Journal* 16.2 (Dec. 1972): 188-97.
        Describes *Les Blancs*, *The Drinking Gourd*, and *What Use Are Flowers* in terms of plot and theme. Relates some background information concerning Robert Nemiroff's involvement in editing the three plays for production.

S32   Potter, Velma R. "New Politics, New Mothers." *CLA Journal* 16.2 (Dec. 1972): 247-55.
        Says that while earlier black drama, like *A Raisin in the Sun*, is optimistic about the larger American society, "and the possibility that even encrusted evil can be scraped, [t]he revolutionary drama of the 60's is not so sanguine about the efficacy of protest or even the vitality of American idealism."

S33   Ness, David E. "Lorraine Hansberry's *Les Blancs*: The Victory of the Man Who Must." *Freedomways* 13.4 (1973): 294-306.
        The play is about Tshembe's change to a com-

mitment to his people that may result in his own death, and this is "one of the most profound and heroic victories of our modern literature." When he kills Abioseh, "who represents a slave-like service of the interests of the exploiters," he is victorious in "making peace with the forces that live and grow by destroying his people."

S34   Phillips, Elizabeth C. *The Works of Lorraine Hansberry [Monarch Notes]*. New York: Simon and Schuster, 1973.

Includes an overview of Hansberry's life and career; a discussion of her themes and style; a selected bibliography; and critical reviews of her periodical articles, public addresses, and plays.

S35   Hay, Samuel A. "African-American Drama, 1950-1970." *Negro History Bulletin* 36 (Jan. 1973): 5-8.

Hails *A Raisin in the Sun* as one of those plays that show "ultimate victory" as a major theme in their portrayal of the African-American experience.

S36   Jones, Clarence B. "The Black Artist Legacy." *New York Amsterdam News* 9 June 1973: A4.

Says Hansberry said she wrote *A Raisin in the Sun* because she was "'tired of seeing Black life misrepresented on the stage in terms of exotic, squalid, and sexually debasing stereotypes having little relationship to the struggle and laughter and strength of our people.'"

S37   Peterson, Maurice. "*Raisin*: A Play with Nine Lives?" *Essence* 4 (Dec. 1973): 15.

Praises the musical for showing that Hansberry's work has "not faded with the years." The "show...comes across powerfully."

S38   Brown, Lloyd W. "Lorraine Hansberry as Ironist: A Reappraisal of *A Raisin in the Sun*." *Journal of Black Studies* 4 (March 1974): 237-47.

Reviews   how   Hansberry   has   become   a

"controversial" artist in terms of her place in the black political spectrum. Suggests that such critics of Hansberry and *A Raisin in the Sun* as Harold Cruse and C.W.E. Bigsby have missed the irony and ambiguity in her portrayal of the American propensity "to confuse material achievement with the total promise of the American dream."

S39   Willis, Robert J. "Anger in the Contemporary Black Theatre." *Negro American Literature Forum* 8 (Summer 1974): 213-15.

Says *A Raisin in the Sun* was "something new and honest" on the New York stage, but that it was also "a warning." Others "would take up, with more anger and less sentimentality," what Hansberry had begun in her forging of a Black consciousness.

S40   Lamb, Margaret. "Feminist Criticism." *Drama Review* 18 (Sept. 1974): 46-50.

Laments, along with the reviewer of the musical *Raisin* in *Ms.* magazine, how important women's issues in the original play are not to be found in the musical. Suggests serious work by and about women is up against a masculine attitude in the theater that may neither appreciate nor promote it.

S41   Bonin, Jane F. *Major Themes in Prize-Winning American Drama.* Metuchen, NJ: Scarecrow, 1975.

Highlights the major ideas and characters in *A Raisin in the Sun.*

S42   Guttmann, Allen. "Integration and 'Black Nationalism' in the Plays of Lorraine Hansberry." *American Drama and Theater in the 20th Century.* Eds. Alfred Weber and Sigfried Neuweiler.   Gottingen: Vandenhoeck and Ruprecht, 1975. 248-60.

Examines *A Raisin in the Sun* and *The Sign in Sidney Brustein's Window* in light of the tension in the African-American community between black nationalists (supporters of racial separation) and exponents of racial integration (where Hansberry "undoubtedly stood"). All in all, with a "good deal of reluctance, one has to admit that the 'black rage' surrealistically embodied in the revolutionary plays of LeRoi Jones leads us to deeper knowledge than that contained in Lorraine Hansberry's quieter forms of protest."

S43   Edward, Sr. Ann. "Three Views on Blacks: The Black Woman in American Literature." *CEA Critic* 37.4 (May 1975): 14-16.

Cites Hansberry as a writer of "high renown" and praises *A Raisin in the Sun*, the character of "Mama" in particular.

S44   Katz, Jonathan. *Gay American History: Lesbians and Gay Men in the U.S.A.--A Documentary.* New York: Thomas Crowell, 1976. 420-33.

S45   Friedberg, Maurice. "The U.S. and the U.S.S.R.: American Literature Through the Filter of Recent Soviet Publishing and Criticism." *Critical Inquiry* 2.3 (Spring 1976): 519-83.

Mentions that *A Raisin in the Sun* was praised for its portrayal of the awakening of the "black's sense of human dignity," and notes that American black authors are "treated with more tolerance than their white colleagues."

S46   Molette, Barbara. "They Speak, Who Listens?: Black Women Playwrights." *Black World* 25.6 (April 1976): 28-34.

Decries the fact that the works of black women playwrights are at the mercy of mostly white media brokers who are not inclined to present "informative entertainment...that might be of some use to an oppressed group." Notes that Hansberry's *Follow the Drinking Gourd [The Drinking Gourd]* was not produced because she shows slavery as "evil, inhuman, and the slavers as barbaric."

S47   Anderson, Mary Louise.   "Black Matriarchy: Portrayals of
       Women in Three Plays." *Negro American Literature
       Forum* 10.3 (Fall 1976): 93-94.
                A Raisin in the Sun is about matriarchy. Mama
       is "the matriarchal stereotype," and her ever-present plant
       symbolizes this.

S48   Hatch, James. "Speak to Me in Those Old Words, You Know,
       Those La-La Words, Those Tung-Tung Sounds (Some
       African Influences on the Afro-American Theatre)." *Yale
       Theatre* 8 (Fall 1976): 25-34.
                Pointing out that most African heritage on the
       American stage in the thirties and forties was "embodied
       in the musical," asserts Hansberry's *A Raisin in the Sun*
       was a giant step "toward creating a particularized Afri-
       can," as she did in *Les Blancs.* Yet "the more Ms. Hans-
       berry succeeded in particularizing the African, the more
       perfectly he spoke the King's English; the more she dis-
       pelled romanticism, the more the kinship of the American
       Express Card superseded ethnic ties."

S49   Oliver, Kitty. "Lorraine Hansberry." *Miami Herald* 16 Dec.
       1976.
                An essay that quotes Robert Nemiroff discussing
       his life with Hansberry, pointing out her concerns as an
       artist and a black activist.

S50   Dodson, Owen. "Who Has Seen the Wind? Playwrights and the
       Black Experience." *Black American Literature Forum*
       11.3 (1977): 108-16.
                A Raisin in the Sun is a play about an ethnic
       group that is "universal and everlasting."

S51   Miller, Jeanne-Marie A. "Images of Black Women in Plays by
       Black Playwrights." *CLA Journal* 20 (June 1977): 494-
       507.
                Discusses Hansberry's never-produced television
       play about slavery, *The Drinking Gourd.* While Rissa
       has some of the characteristics of the "unrealistic

mammy," she is also concerned about her own family. In various actions, Hansberry's slave mother "reverses the myth of the faithful, contented slave," who is happy in her servitude. Ultimately riveting her attention on her son, Rissa lets her master die outside her cabin.

S52   Powell, Bertie J. "The Black Experience in Margaret Walker's *Jubilee* and Lorraine Hansberry's *The Drinking Gourd*." *CLA Journal* 21.2 (Dec. 1977): 304-11.

While *The Drinking Gourd* depicts the black experience during the times of slavery, it also reveals how some white people "were caught up with the evils of slavery by virtue of their existence in a slave culture," but still "refused to permit the system to destroy their humanity." Discusses the play's focus on white and black characters' views of slavery.

S53   Marill, Alvin H. *The Films of Sidney Poitier*. Secaucus, NJ: Citadel, 1978. 97-100.

Reviews the major themes of *A Raisin in the Sun* and includes some production information about the film along with several photos.

S54   Scanlan, Tom. *Family, Drama, and American Dream*. Westport: Greenwood, 1978. 195-201.

Cites *A Raisin in the Sun* as the "best" of the newer plays concerned with the black family. "Like Odets, Hansberry writes a realistic social drama of the struggle for life by little people...." The play revolves around a "conflict between security and freedom," Hansberry exploring the "creative possibilities along with the destructive side" of this conflict.

S55   Scheader, Catherine. *They Found a Way: Lorraine Hansberry*. Chicago: Children's Press, 1978.

A book for young people that outlines Hansberry's life and how her family taught her great pride in being black as well as a will to succeed. Includes family photos and some of Hansberry's own drawings.

S56   Baldwin, James. "Lorraine Hansberry at the Summit." *Free-domways* 19.4 (1979): 269-72.
       Recounts with deep admiration Hansberry's articulate and moving confrontation with Attorney General Robert Kennedy over civil rights issues in New York on May 24, 1963.

S57   Bennett, Lerone Jr. and Margaret C. Burroughs. "A Lorraine Hansberry Rap." *Freedomways* 19.4 (1979): 226-33.
       A discussion between the authors about such subjects as Hansberry's background, artistic life, social concerns, politics, and feminism.

S58   Bond, Jean Carey. "Lorraine Hansberry: To Reclaim Her Legacy." *Freedomways* 19.4 (1979): 183-85.
       Introduces a series of essays in this issue of *Freedomways*, which was devoted solely to Lorraine Hansberry.

S59   Carter, Steven R. "The John Brown Theatre: Lorraine Hansberry's Cultural Views and Dramatic Goals." *Freedomways* 19.4 (1979): 186-91.
       Recounts a community theater project, conceived by Hansberry two years before her death. Notes that naming the black community theater after a white man emphasized the paradoxical nature of Hansberry's world view and art. She was a "fighter for her race who insisted on 'the oneness of the cause of humanity'...A Pan-Africanist who wished to place the Western heritage of Afro-Americans alongside the African heritage; a revolutionary dramatist who strove to be an artist as well as a propagandist."

S60   Elder, Lonne III. "Lorraine Hansberry: Social Consciousness and the Will." *Freedomways* 19.4 (1979): 213-18.
       Hansberry's was "a perennial struggle to be engaged by the events and issues convulsing the world, on the one hand; but on the other, to--necessarily and simultaneously--prompt her will to *disengage* the social re-

sponsibility which is necessary to rectify the world's infirmities." Discusses *A Raisin in the Sun* and *The Sign in Sidney Brustein's Window*.

S61   Giovanni, Nikki. "An Emotional View of Lorraine Hansberry." *Freedomways* 19.4 (1979): 281-82.

Hansberry was one of those "wonderful human beings who, seeing both sides of the dilemma and all sides of the coin, still called 'Heads' when she tossed."

S62   Gresham, Jewell Handy. "Lorraine Hansberry as Prose Stylist." *Freedomways* 19.4 (1979): 192-204.

Hansberry has been rightfully credited as "the Mother of modern black drama." Yet she should also be celebrated for her "classical artistry as a prose stylist." Discusses her essays and portions of *To Be Young, Gifted and Black* to demonstrate her mastery of the essay form.

S63   Haley, Alex. "The Once and Future Vision of Lorraine Hansberry." *Freedomways* 19.4 (1979): 227-80.

Comments on *A Raisin in the Sun*, *The Sign in Sidney Brustein's Window*, and *Les Blancs* to demonstrate Hansberry's exquisite sense of social and historical change. While she was not the first black writer to "illuminate the relationship between the American Black and Africa...she was the first to *popularize* the notion."

S64   Killens, John Oliver. "Lorraine Hansberry: On Time." *Freedomways* 19.4 (1979): 273-76.

Asserts that Hansberry was a writer who wrote to cause change. She "was an extraordinarily articulate young black woman, committed to the struggle and very fast on the draw. Indeed, literarily and intellectually, she was one of the fastest guns in the East--and her gun was for revolution and for change."

S65   King, Woodie Jr. "Lorraine Hansberry's Children: Black Artists and *A Raisin in the Sun*." *Freedomways* 19.4 (1979): 219-22.

Recounts how the "doors" within the author's "consciousness" were opened with his viewing of *A Raisin in the Sun* in 1959. In making his film, *The Black Theater Movement: A Raisin in the Sun to the Present*, over 40 people interviewed said they had been influenced or aided by Hansberry's work.

S66   Mayfield, Julian. "Lorraine Hansberry: A Woman For All Seasons." *Freedomways* 19.4 (1979): 263-68.

Reminisces about Lorraine Hansberry's social and political concerns, citing several incidents and experiences that demonstrated her commitment to the causes of civil rights and black identity.

S67   Rahman, Aishah. "To Be Black, Female and a Playwright." *Freedomways* 19.4 (1979): 256-60.

Rejects the complaints of the Black activists of 1959 about *A Raisin in the Sun* being a bourgeois drama that made "white folks feel comfortable at black expense." Finds it ironic that the "Black Arts Movement" that Hansberry's play helped usher in, itself "debased black female identity" with plays by black men who found the character of the strong black female an image of male enslavement.

S68   Rich, Adrienne. "The Problem with Lorraine Hansberry." *Freedomways* 19.4 (1979): 247-55.

Finds the works complied and edited by Robert Nemiroff after Hansberry's death "a problem" in terms of who is really the author. Ponders the female characters in the plays and finds there are no "revolutionary, confrontational" figures who, unlike Mama in *A Raisin in the Sun* are "both angry and sexual." Regrets Hansberry's apparent repression or censorship of lesbian and women's concerns that might have been an important part of her drama.

S69   Riley, Clayton. "Lorraine Hansberry: A Melody in a Different Key." *Freedomways* 19.4 (1979): 205-12.

Reviews major themes of *A Raisin in the Sun*, *The Sign in Sidney Brustein's Window*, *Les Blancs*, and *The Drinking Gourd* as examples of how Hansberry's art offered "a portrait of life that may be harsh and disillusioning" with "adversary forces that can and must be encountered and, ultimately,...overcome."

S70   Royals, Demetria Brendan. "The Me Lorraine Hansberry Knew." *Freedomways* 19.4 (1979): 261-62.

Tells how the author, herself young, gifted and black, found out who she was by reading *A Raisin in the Sun*.

S71   Ward, Douglas Turner. "Lorraine Hansberry and the Passion of Walter Lee." *Freedomways* 19.4 (1979): 223-25.

Those who find Walter Lee in *A Raisin in the Sun* a "repository of all the negative, materialist aspirations of American society" hold a "tremendously simplistic" view of the character and the play. Walter Lee is a complex "bearer of aims and goals that have been conditioned by the prevailing values of the society...." He is "flawed, contradictory, irascible, impulsive, furious...and desperate." He is the black man ready to explode.

S72   Wilkerson, Margaret B. "Lorraine Hansberry: The Complete Feminist." *Freedomways* 19.4 (1979): 235-45.

Notes that with her statement, "'I was born black and a female,'" Hansberry immediately established the "basis for a tension" that informed her world view. Her consciousness of both "ethnicity and gender...brought awareness of two key forces of conflict and oppression in the contemporary world." Discusses Mama in *A Raisin in the Sun* and Rissa in *The Drinking Gourd* as examples of Hansberry's concern with feminist issues.

S73   Wright, Sarah E. "Lorraine Hansberry on Film." *Freedomways* 19.4 (1979): 283-84.

Celebrates the documentary film on Hansberry's

life and career, "Lorraine Hansberry: The Black Experience in the Creation of Drama," which premiered in May,
1979.

S74   Donohue, John W. "Bench Marks." *America* 140.2 (20 Jan.
1979): 30-33.
                 Recounts Hansberry's, and other black intel-
lectuals', May 24, 1963 meeting with then Attorney General Robert Kennedy, who seemed unable to understand
their concerns and problems. Outlines Hansberry's life,
and includes comment on her religious perspective which
is described as not being "hostile" to religion "unless it
happened to be Catholic." Suggests she "replaced Christianity with a thin version of scientific humanism."

S75   Hairston, Loyle. "Lorraine Hansberry--Portrait of an Angry
Young Writer." *Crisis* 86.4 (April 1979): 123-28.
                 Reviews how Hansberry's political and social
concerns grew out of her experiences working in Harlem
on Paul Robeson's radical weekly, *Freedom*; her appreciation of the ideas of W.E.B. Du Bois; and her inspira-
tion by Irish playwright Sean O'Casey.

S76   Walker, Alice. "One Child of One's Own." *Ms.* (magazine) 8.2
(Aug. 1979): 72-73.
                 Discusses the author's experiences of giving birth
and finding her voice as a writer. Mentions reading she
found essential, including the work of women writers like
Lorraine Hansberry (*To Be Young, Gifted and Black* in
particular) which show "black women as *women*."

1980-1989

S77   Mael, Phyllis. "Beyond Hellman and Hansberry: The Impact of
Feminism on a Decade of Drama by Women." *Kansas
Quarterly* 12.4 (1980): 141-44.
                 The essay deals with women dramatists of the
1970's who have proliferated in the male-dominated field
since the time of Hansberry.

S78   Carter, Steven R. "Commitment and Complexity: Lorraine Hansberry's Life in Action." *Melus* 7.3 (Fall 1980): 39-53.

In order to correct published mistakes concerning Hansberry's life and career, includes an accurate chronology of her life. Reviews her artistic accomplishments and her political/social perspectives.

S79   Adams, Michael. "Lorraine Hansberry." *Dictionary of Literary Biography.* Ed. John MacNicholas. Detroit: Gale, 1981. 247-54.

S80   Keyssar, Helene. *The Curtain and the Veil: Strategies in Black Drama.* New York: Burt Franklin, 1981. 113-46.

In a chapter titled "Sounding the Rumble of Dreams Deferred: Lorraine Hansberry's *A Raisin in the Sun*," asserts that the play "dramatizes the efforts and frustrations of a family in pursuit of the American dream." In a larger historical context, the play is the best known of the black dramas "that transforms into theatrical terms the political strategy of integration."

S81   Olauson, Judith. *The American Woman Playwright: A View of Criticism and Characterization.* Troy, NY: Whitston, 1981. 89+.

An overview of themes and characterization in *A Raisin in the Sun* and *The Sign in Sidney Brustein's Window.*

S82   Davis, Arthur P. *From the Dark Tower: Afro-American Writers 1900-1960.* Washington DC: Howard UP, 1982. 203-7.

Briefly reviews Hansberry's dramatic works in light of her commitment to her race.

S83   Greenfield, Thomas Allen. *Work and the Work Ethic in American Drama, 1920-1970.* Columbia, MO: U of Missouri P, 1982. 131-41.

Asserts that *A Raisin in the Sun* is significant as

an exploration of the variety of attitudes about work that are reflective of black life in America. The play "examines differences between older rural blacks and younger urban blacks, the tensions between educated and uneducated blacks, and it presents a credible picture of a crisis in self-image among black males...."

S84   Schiff, Ellen. *From Stereotype of Metaphor: The Jew in Contemporary Drama*. Albany: SUNY P, 1982. 156-60.

Asserts that a "sensitive concept of the Jewish experience as archetypal" is a subtext of Hansberry's *The Sign in Sidney Brustein's Window*. Brustein is "the Jew who has found his niche in society and occupies it with the same aplomb with which he wears his identity." Because he has known prejudice and rejection, he relates to all, regardless of race, sex, or social status. He is not just the Jew making his way in a hostile society and helping others as he goes along, but is also "unaccommodated man, determined to shape his world to more human proportions."

S85   McGovern, Edythe M. "Lorraine Hansberry." *American Women Writers: A Critical Reference Guide from Colonial Times to the Present*. Ed. Langdon Lynne Faust. New York: Frederick Unger, 1983. 291-93.

S86   Wilkerson, Margaret B. "The Sighted Eyes and Feeling Heart of Lorraine Hansberry." *Black American Literature Forum* 17.1 (Spring 1983): 8-13.

Reviews the major themes and ideas of Hansberry's plays. Asserts that only "in hindsight do we now realize that [she] heralded the new [Black Arts Movement of the 1960's] and, in fact, became one of its major literary catalysts."

S87   Cheney, Anne. *Lorraine Hansberry*. Boston: Twayne, 1984.

A comprehensive study of Lorraine Hansberry including an extensive biographical overview, chapters on the major dramatic works, and a selected bibliography.

S88   Friedman, Sharon. "Feminism as Theme in Twentieth-Century
       Women's Drama." *American Studies* 25.1 (1984): 69-
       89.

       In periods when women's equality has been a
powerful social issue, feminist concerns are central to
plays by women. Lena in *A Raisin in the Sun* and Rissa
in *The Drinking Gourd* are not dramatizations of black
women who emasculate black men. Rather, Hansberry's
"mothers...repudiate the negative images of black women
as passive and/or destructive." They are women "who
contribute not only to the survival of their families and
communities, but also to the active resistance often necessary to that survival."

S89   Norment, Lynn. "*Raisin* Celebrates Its 25th Anniversary."
       Ebony 39.5 (March 1984): 57-60.

       Mentions how the original *A Raisin in the Sun*
launched the careers of some great actors and highlights
the celebrations taking place across the nation on the 25th
Anniversary revival of the play. The play "accentuates
Black pride and the courage to fight White racism...[and]
addresses a woman's role in the home and the work
place."

S90   Rahman, Aishah. "First Light of a New Day." *In These Times*
       8.17 (1984): 8-9.

       Reviews Hansberry's career, asserting that her
works deal with such contemporary issues as "the disen-
gagement of the American liberal, sexism, colonialism,
capitalism vs. socialism, war and peace and the survival
of our planet." Argues that she was a "conscious feminist," a supporter of the "early gay rights movement,"
and a "dedicated socialist."

S91   Salaam, Kalamu ya. "What Use Is Writing: Re-Reading Lor-
       raine Hansberry." *Black Collegian* 4.4 (March/April
       1984): 45-47.

       Hansberry has not been properly recognized
because, among other things, she was "middle class when

the [Black] movement concentrated on 'authenticity' of
the poor and unemployed Black," and "she was married
to a white man and was therefore automatically rejected."
Reviews Hansberry's relevance as an African-American
artist and includes some of her early poems.

S92   Sequeira, Isaac. "Images of Black Culture in Modern American
       Drama." *Journal of American Culture* 7.1/2 (Spring/
       Summer 1984): 45-48.
              Takes issue with scholars who claim that blacks
       in America do not have a culture separate and distinct
       from the main stream of American culture. Cites how
       jazz and the blues, distinctions of the black American
       culture, pervade *The Sign in Sidney Brustein's Window*,
       even though the play does not deal with a racial situation;
       and how *A Raisin in the Sun* demonstrates "humor for its
       own sake and as a survival strategy," another example of
       the black experience.

S93   Nemiroff, Robert. "From These Roots: Lorraine Hansberry and
       the South." *Southern Exposure* Sept./Oct. 1984: 32-36.
              Discusses Hansberry's interest in the South and
       slavery, mentioning her unfinished novel, *All the Dark
       and Beautiful Warriors* and NBC's refusal to produce
       The Drinking Gourd. Also includes a review of her
       achievement in the civil rights movement.

S94   Carter, Steven R. "Images of Men in Lorraine Hansberry's
       Writing." *Black American Literature Forum* 19.4
       (1985): 160-62.
              Relates Hansberry's commitment to a feminist
       perspective and her strident support of women's rights.
       Yet asserts that she created many sympathetic male char-
       acters because she felt to the "'extent that the Feminist
       leaders pronounced *man* rather than ideology as enemy
       they deserved correction.'" Hansberry saw her male
       characters caught in the same cultural web of "male su-
       premacy," as her females and dramatized the "resulting
       harm they do to women and themselves."

S95   Christian, Barbara. *Black Feminist Criticism*. New York:
       Pergamon, 1985. 199.

              In a discussion of lesbianism and feminism, cites
       Hansberry's "Letter to *The Ladder*" which expresses
       hope that there "may be women who emerge who will be
       able to formulate a new and possible concept that homo-
       sexual condemnation has at its roots not only social igno-
       rance but a philosophically active anti-feminist dogma."

S96   Wilkerson, Margaret B. "Diverse Angles of Vision: Two Black
       Women Playwrights." *Theatre Annual* 40 (1985): 91-
       114.

              Both Lorraine Hansberry and Adrienne Kennedy
       have been "bombarded by the cruelties and absurdities of
       racism and sexism...." And both "use the social and po-
       litical experience as singular reference points for their re-
       flections on important human issues." Recounts the
       playwrights' differences in approach, focusing on *A Rai-
       sin in the Sun* and *The Sign in Sidney Brustein's Window*
       in terms of Hansberry.

S97   Barthelemy, Anthony. "Mother, Sister, Wife: A Dramatic Per-
       spective." *Southern Review* 21.3 (1985): 770-89.

              Describes how Hansberry's feminist vision in *A
       Raisin in the Sun* is a response to Theodore Ward's 1938
       play *Big White Fog*. Hansberry seeks to "correct Ward's
       presentation of black women and to place black political
       aspirations firmly within the traditional American bour-
       geois context by countering the revolutionary Marxist
       politics of *Big White Fog*."

S98   Brown-Guillory, Elizabeth. "Lorraine Hansberry: The Politics of
       the Politics Surrounding *The Drinking Gourd*." *Griot*
       4.1/2 (Summer/Winter 1985): 18-28.

              Asserts that Hansberry was both "artistic and
       political." Examines the reception of *The Drinking
       Gourd* and how "Hansberry's writing of political plays
       opened up the door for other playwrights who saw no di-
       chotomy between art and politics."

S99   Coles, Robert. *The Moral Life of Children*. Boston: Houghton,
         1986. 60.
                 Speaking of the African-American family, refers
         to the Youngers in *A Raisin in the Sun* as examples of
         people living in a "continual tension between hope and
         despair...whose prospects are by no means cheerful."

S100   Bennett, Lerone Jr. "The Ten Biggest Myths About the Black
         Family." *Ebony* August 1986: 123+.
                 Seeks to debunk the "myths and outright lies men
         and women have invented to hide themselves from Black
         reality and American racism." Cites *A Raisin in the Sun*
         as rightfully demonstrating that the myth of a family
         structure of domineering black women and "weak and ab-
         sent" black men is an oversimplification. Mama actually
         celebrates the strength and love of her late husband as he
         faced his, and his family's, hard life with "a love and a
         strength beyond history and beyond understanding...."

S101   Wilkerson, Margaret B. *"A Raisin in the Sun*: Anniversary of an
         American Classic." *Theatre Journal* 38.4 (Dec. 1986):
         441-52.
                 Reviews the major themes of the play along with
         critical reaction to the original and subsequent produc-
         tions of the play. Notes the factors that mark the play a
         "classic."

S102   Alder, Thomas P. *Mirror on the Stage: The Pulitzer Plays As
         an Approach to American Drama*. West Lafayette, IN:
         . Purdue UP, 1987.
                 Observes that Hansberry's *A Raisin in the Sun*
         upset many blacks by not "questioning critically enough
         whether the dream that her protagonist pursues has been
         irreparably tainted by white values." The play examines
         "the ethic that equates 'being somebody' with material
         success while urging a new generation of black men to
         achieve dignity by coming into their own as husbands and
         fathers."

S103   Barka, Amiri (LeRoi Jones). *"A Raisin in the Sun's* Enduring
        Passion." *A Raisin in the Sun* (Unabridged 25th Anni-
        versary Edition) *and The Sign in Sidney Brustein's Win-
        dow.* Ed. Robert Nemiroff. New York: Plume, 1987.
        9-20.
                Celebrates *A Raisin in the Sun* as a work of
        critical realism that moves beyond mere realism in its
        most limited form. That is, Hansberry *"analyzes and as-
        sesses* reality and shapes her statement as an aesthetically
        powerful and politically advanced work of art." Notes
        how restored passages point to her concerns with con-
        temporary issues such as political agitation, black power,
        and "neo-colonialism and the growth (and corruption) of
        a post-colonial African bourgeoisie--'the servants of em-
        pire,'" as one of the characters calls them.

S104   Berrian, Brenda F. "The Afro-American-West African Marriage
        Question: Its Literary and Historical Contexts." *Women
        in African Literature Today.* Ed. Durosimi Jones.
        Trenton: Africa World, 1987. 152-59.
                Focuses on the theme of interracial marriage
        between Beneatha and Joseph Asagai in *A Raisin in the
        Sun* which "can be viewed as a testimony of self-affirma-
        tion, new freedom and a positive step towards black
        identity."

S105   Braine, John. *"Sidney Brustein--A 'Great'* Play--No Other Word
        Possible." *A Raisin in the Sun* (Unabridged 25th Anni-
        versary Edition) *and The Sign in Sidney Brustein's Win-
        dow.* Ed. Robert Nemiroff. New York: Plume, 1987.
        155-59.
                Applauds the play for its blunt honesty that
        caused many to criticize it. Defending Hansberry's
        treatment of the homosexual character that brought her
        criticism, says that it is seemingly fine "for an audience to
        be asked to sympathize with a homosexual's sad pre-
        dicament," but it is a different matter when we are shown,
        as we are in Hansberry's play, that homosexuals "are not
        only victims but make others victims...that homosexuality

is not a special order but a form of sex."

S106   Nemiroff, Robert. Foreword. *A Raisin in the Sun* (Unabridged
       25th Anniversary Edition) *and The Sign in Sidney
       Brustein's Window*. New York: Plume, 1987. ix-xviii.
           Discusses the scenes and lines restored to this
       "anniversary edition" of *A Raisin in the Sun*, pointing out
       that they emphasize such issues as "women's conscious-
       ness" and the "revolutionary ferment in Africa." A num-
       ber of the excised passages speak directly to such con-
       temporary issues as "value systems of the black family
       and the conflict between generations," including concepts
       of African-American beauty, identity, and hairstyle, as
       well as observations concerning the relationships between
       black men and women, husbands and wives.

S107   Rich, Frank. "An Appreciation: *A Raisin in the Sun*--The 25th
       Anniversary." *A Raisin in the Sun* (Unabridged 25th
       Anniversary Edition) *and The Sign in Sidney Brustein's
       Window*. Ed. Robert Nemiroff. New York: Plume,
       1987. 7-8.
           Affectionately acknowledges Hansberry's
       achievement with *A Raisin in the Sun*, noting how the
       play today resembles works of other Chicago writers
       "from Dreiser's *Sister Carrie* to David Ma-
       met's... *American Buffalo*."

S108   Brown-Guillory, Elizabeth. "Black Women Playwrights: Exor-
       cising Myths." *Phylon* 48.3 (Fall 1987): 229-39.
           Discusses the works of Alice Childress, Ntozake
       Shange, and Lorraine Hansberry and how their
       "perspectives and portraits are decidedly different from
       those of black males and white playwrights...." These
       women have worked to "dispel the myths of the
       'contented slave,' 'the tragic mulatto,' 'the comic Negro,'
       'the exotic primitive,' and the 'spiritual singing, toe-tap-
       ping, faithful servant.'" Focuses on *A Raisin in the Sun*.

S109   Wilkerson, Margaret B. "The Dark Vision of Lorraine Hansberry: Excerpts from a Literary Biography." *Massachusetts Review* 28.4 (Winter 1987): 642-50.

 Notes that while Hansberry has been applauded as a playwright of "hope and commitment," in fact "hers was a dark vision that celebrated the potential of human beings while recognizing the stark realities of man's inhumanity to man....She felt deeply the legacy of slavery that haunts the American experience." She is of interest to scholars who find meaningful complexity in her homosexuality and feminism.

S110 Brown-Guillory, Elizabeth. *Their Place on the Stage: Black Women Playwrights in America.* New York: Greenwood, 1988.

 Reviews aspects of Hansberry's life and career including the major themes of her dramatic works.

S111 Rousuck, J. Wynn. "Former Critics Now See 1959 Play as a Classic." *Baltimore Sun* 24 April 1988.

 Relates how those critical of the original production of *A Raisin in the Sun*, such as Amiri Baraka (LeRoi Jones) and George C. Wolfe (who satirized the play and Hansberry in his drama, *The Colored Museum*), now find it praiseworthy.

S112 Carter, Steven R. "Colonialism and Culture in Lorraine Hansberry's *Les Blancs*." *Melus* 15.1 (Spring 1988): 27-45.

 Notes the similarities and parallels between Shakespeare's *Hamlet* and her play to demonstrate Hansberry's view of colonialism and its national and personal consequences. *Les Blancs* is "one of the most scathing and enduring indictments of colonialism and all similar social injustices, both from a European and African standpoint."

S113 Washington, Charles J. *"A Raisin in the Sun Revisited." Black American Literature Forum* 22.1 (Spring 1988): 109-24.

 Reviews criticisms of the play as a mere "social

drama," and argues for its "greatness and universality."
Walter is a "tragic hero" and a "realistic hero" who is
elevated by his "growth from ignorance to knowledge."
By the drama's ending, Walter and his family are as
"poor and powerless as they were before," but while their
lives are essentially unchanged, the new house provides a
"pinch of dignity."

S114   Carter, Steven R.   "Inter-ethnic Issues in Lorraine Hansberry's
        The Sign in Sidney Brustein's Window." *Explorations in
        Ethnic Studies: The Journal of the National Association
        for Ethnic Studies* 11.2 (July 1988): 1-13.
                While some critics lament that Hansberry did not
        focus on the black experience in her play, this criticism is
        unjust since *The Sign in Sidney Brustein's Window* ex-
        plores many of the same issues as *A Raisin in the Sun.*
        Both grapple with the "oppressive system that enables
        some to live in luxury while the many just survive," a
        system that "strives to wipe out ethnic cultures as poten-
        tial sources of resistance through the concept of the
        'melting pot.'"   Of Sidney's harsh remarks to/about
        David, the homosexual, Carter suggests that they dem-
        onstrate how hard it is for people (even liberals like Sid-
        ney), to divorce themselves from the prejudices ingrained
        in them by their cultures.   Likens the Black to the Jewish
        experience.

S115   Keyssar, Helene.   "Rites and Responsibilities: The Drama of
        Black American Women."   *Feminine Focus: The New
        Women Playwrights.*   Ed. Enoch Brater.   New York:
        Oxford UP, 1989.   226-40.
                A discussion of plays by black American women
        which "suggest the potential power in the matching of
        theater and black consciousness."   In *A Raisin in the Sun*,
        Hansberry "constructed a dramatic world in which the
        wit and charm of the characters [unfortunately] distracted
        the audience from the dangers and contradictions of the
        social world they inhabited...."

S116   Wilkerson, Margaret B. "Lorraine Hansberry." *Notable Women in the American Theatre: A Biographical Dictionary.* Eds. Alice Robinson, Vera Mowry Roberts, Milly S. Barranger. New York: Greenwood, 1989. 374-80.

S117   Woll, Allen. *Black Musical Theatre: From Coontown to Dreamgirls.* Baton Rouge: Louisiana State UP, 1989. 261-63.

       Reviews the origin and production of the musical *Raisin.*

S118   Peerman, Dean. *"A Raisin in the Sun:* The Uncut Version." *Christian Century* 25 Jan. 1989: 71-73.

       Notes that Hansberry was "astounded" that critics of the original 1959 production thought the play had a happy ending, and asserts that the new 1989 PBS American Playhouse production would remedy such misinterpretations with restorations of portions cut from the original.

S119   Hooks, Bell. *"Raisin* in a New Light." *Christianity and Crisis* 6 Feb. 1989: 21-23.

       An essay welcoming the new 1989 PBS production of *A Raisin in the Sun* that claims that the new production, which restores cut portions of the play, moves beyond the family's concerns over money to the playwright's ideas about "U.S. imperialism, colonialism, African independence, and the changing status of women."

S120   Carter, Steven R. "Lorraine Hansberry's *Toussaint.*" *Black American Literature Forum* 23.1 (Spring 1989): 139-48.

       Reviews the fragments of Hansberry's unfinished play and its various levels of significance. Quotes Hansberry as saying in regard to the work, that an "'oppressive society will dehumanize and degenerate everyone involved--and in certain very poetic and very true ways at the same time it will tend to make...the oppressed have

more stature--because at least they are arbitrarily placed
in the situation of overwhelming that which is degenerate...'"

1990-1996

S121   Ashley, Leonard R.N. "Lorraine Hansberry and the Great Black
       Way." *Modern American Drama: The Female Canon.*
       Ed. June Schlueter. Madison: Fairleigh Dickinson UP,
       1990. 151-60.
            An overview of Hansberry's career as a play-
       wright with brief reviews of the critical receptions of each
       of her plays. Mentions that her papers contain "a novel,
       a screenplay based on the Haitian novelist Jacques Rou-
       main's *Masters of the Dew*, and political articles and
       dramatic fragments, including *The Arrival of Mr. Todog*,
       a skit satirizing *Waiting for Godot.*"

S122   Gomez, Jewelle L. "Lorraine Hansberry: Uncommon Warrior."
       *Reading Black, Reading Feminist: A Critical Anthol-
       ogy.* Ed. Henry Louis Gates, Jr. New York: Meridian,
       1990. 307-17.
            Applauds Hansberry's political activism from the
       vantage point of the 1990's. Notes her political and so-
       cial radicalism and her championship of the rights of
       women and gays. "Because we have not studied Hans-
       berry as a cultural worker and thinker but only as a
       dramatist, we have lost touch with the urgency of her
       political message...."

S123   Richards, Dell. *Lesbian Lists: A Look at Lesbian Culture,
       History, and Personalities.* Boston: Alyson, 1990. 32.

S124   Russell, Sandi. *Render Me My Song: African-American Women
       Writers from Slavery to the Present.* New York: St.
       Martin's, 1990. 54-56.
            Notes that *A Raisin in the Sun* demonstrates
       Hansberry's "deft orchestration of a variety of complex
       themes": the "portrayal of the African-American family,

their lifestyles, speech-patterns, wit and strength coupled with theories of Pan-Africanism."

S125   Wilkerson, Margaret B. "Excavating Our History: The Importance of Biographies of Women of Color." *Black American Literature Forum* 24.1 (1990): 73-84.

Recounts how the author's respect for the work of the biographer has grown as she, herself, works on biographies of Lorraine Hansberry and Louise Thompson Patterson. Notes her discovery of Hansberry's complexity in terms of politics and sexuality. In her biography, Hansberry's homosexuality "and the contradiction between her own personal preferences and her treatment of the subject in her produced plays made for some important speculation about the nature of her vision."

S126   Spitz, Ellen Handler. "Mothers and Daughters: Ancient and Modern Myths." *Journal of Aesthetics and Art Criticism* 48.4 (Fall 1990): 411-20.

The scene in *A Raisin in the Sun* in which Beneatha challenges her mother's notion of God and is slapped by her mother who "guides, disciplines, supports and opposes her," is compared to the Demeter-Presephone myth in which the girl is "a second edition of her mother, their object relations...deeply structured by this sameness."

S127   Shinn, Thelma J. "Living the Answer: The Emergence of African American Feminist Drama." *Studies in the Humanities* 17.2 (Dec. 1990): 149-59.

Hansberry's commitment to "teach and work" to express her individual perspective of the truth, as dramatized in *A Raisin in the Sun*, provided a model for other African-American playwrights: Adrienne Kennedy, Ntozake Shange, and Alice Childress. Reviews the works of these playwrights as they were affected by Hansberry's.

S128   Carter, Steven R. *Hansberry's Drama: Commitment and*

Complexity. Urbana: U of Illinois P, 1991.

An excellent, comprehensive study of Hansberry's "multicultural dramatic work." Contains an overview of her life and chapters on each of the major dramatic works, with the exception of *To Be Young, Gifted and Black.* Includes discussion of unpublished works, as well.

S129   Shannon, Sandra G.   "From Lorraine Hansberry to August Wilson: An Interview with Lloyd Richards." *Callaloo* 14.1 (1991): 124-35.

Mentions *A Raisin in the Sun* in passing in terms of portrayals of African American women in the modern black theater.

S130   Bigsby, C.W.E. *Modern American Drama, 1945-1990.* London: Cambridge UP, 1991. 269-76.

Compares and contrasts Hansberry's *A Raisin in the Sun* to Miller's *Death of a Salesman.* Hansberry's play leans "into the future" at the level of plot and character. "New commitments and new resources are identified, new sources of energy." In Miller's play, "no such vision is held out." At its heart, *The Sign in Sidney Brustein's Window* is concerned with "commitment in all its guises--political, racial, sexual--and an awareness of betrayal as a central motif of human existence." Mentions *Les Blancs, The Drinking Gourd,* and *Where Are the Flowers* [*What Use Are Flowers*].

S131   Berkowitz, Gerald M. *American Drama of the Twentieth Century.* New York: Longman, 1992. 103-4.

The real insight of *A Raisin in the Sun* is into a "unique tragedy of black family life in America; that generations of racism have damaged the spirit of the men, forcing the women to assume responsibilities that only further the men's emasculation."

S132   James, Rosetta. *Cliffs Notes on Hansberry's "A Raisin in the Sun."* Lincoln, NE: Cliffs Notes, 1992.

Includes sections on the play's characters, a
synopsis of the play, critical commentaries, discussions of
the "three versions" of the play, a review of Hansberry's
life and career, and a selected bibliography.

S133   Katz, Jonathan Ned. *Gay American History: Lesbians and Gay
Men in the U.S.A.*, revised. New York: Meridian, 1992.
425.

In a discussion of the lesbian publication *The
Ladder*, quotes Hansberry's "anonymous" letters to that
periodical which praise its existence and applaud its
feminist perspective.

S134   Marre, Diana. "Lorraine Hansberry." *Notable Black American
Women*. Ed. Jessie Carney Smith. Detroit: Gale, 1992.
452-57.

S135   Seaton, Sandra. *"A Raisin in the Sun*: A Study in Afro-American Culture." *Midwestern Miscellany* 20 (1992): 40-49.

Reviews Harold Cruse's criticism that Hansberry's work fails to dramatize black-nationalist views,
and C.W.E. Bigsby's contention that her play is too spe-
cific to the "plight of the Negro" to express a concern for
humanity at large. Contends, contrary to Cruse and
Bigsby, that *A Raisin in the Sun* is complex, and is true
to the black experience, succeeding as a "work of literature and as a cultural document."

S136   Trudeau, Lawrence J., ed. *Drama Criticism: Criticism of the
Most Significant and Widely Studied Dramatic Works
from All the World's Literatures*. Detroit: Gale, 1992.
239-65.

S137   Thompson, Thelma B. "Character Education For the Twenty-
First Century: Possibilities of a Humanist Curriculum."
CLA Journal 35.3 (March 1992): 263-73.

Cites *A Raisin in the Sun* as a text that dramatizes the importance and process of character education,
which should be a part of our teaching curriculum.

S138   Gruesser, John. "Lies That Kill: Lorraine Hansberry's Answer
           to *Heart of Darkness* in *Les Blancs*." *American Drama*
           1.2 (Spring 1992): 1-14.

                Traces Hansberry's understanding of Africa and
           what it means to be an African-American. Analyzes why
           Les Blancs is her pioneering effort to depict Africa by
           "non-Africanist means." The play attempts to "explode
           the dominant image of Africa by rewriting Joseph Con-
           rad's *Heart of Darkness*, arguably [the] most influential
           (and imitated) Africanist text."

S139   McKelly, James C. "Hymns of Sedition: Portraits of the Artist
           in Contemporary African-American Drama." *Arizona
           Quarterly* 48.1 (Spring 1992): 87-107.

                Hansberry's *A Raisin in the Sun* never strays
           from the "implicit premise that American democratic
           capitalism can be the vehicle of African-American politi-
           cal and economic ascent." Yet by 1962 in *To Be Young,
           Gifted and Black*, Hansberry "contradicted her own role
           as the author of *Raisin*, presenting an artist less amenable
           to the white cultural establishment and, as a result, more
           threatening to white political authority...."

S140   Wilkerson, Margaret B. "Lorraine Hansberry." *African Ameri-
           can Writers*. Eds. Valerie Smith, Lea Baechler, A. Wal-
           ton Litz. New York: Macmillan, 1993. 121-31.

S141   Wilkerson, Margaret B. "Lorraine Vivian Hansberry." *Black
           Women in America: An Historical Encyclopedia*. Ed.
           Darlene Clark Hine. New York: Carlson, 1993. 524-29.

S142   Taylor, Susan L. "Your Spiritual Armor." *Essence* 23.11
           (March 1993): 65.

                Compares Hansberry, who "had to defend herself
           against the white press and against Black intellectuals
           who denigrated her...and accused her of pandering to
           whites," to the first African-American female U.S. sena-
           tor, Carol Mosely Braun.

S143   Cooper, David D. "Hansberry's *A Raisin in the Sun*." *The Explicator* 52.1 (Fall 1993): 59-61.

   With Beneatha's painful awareness that being a doctor won't cure what really ails mankind, the play "pivots delicately on the moral fulcrum...that positions between hope and despair or, put in a socioethical idiom, between idealism and fatalism."

S144   Alder, Thomas P. *American Drama, 1940-1960: A Critical History*. New York: Twayne, 1994. 181-200.

   The chapter, "Lorraine Hansberry: Exploring Dreams, Explosive Drama," surveys the playwright's professional life as one guided by her race and her sex. Discusses the issue of black matriarchy and other feminist issues in *A Raisin in the Sun*. Views *The Sign in Sidney Brustein's Window* as a play "about the need for caring" by people who must battle their cynicism and despair to do so, and *Les Blancs* as an exploration of "the ways in which Christianity, colonialism, and capitalism have conspired to oppress, enslave, and deracinate native Africans."

S145   Berkowitz, Gerald M. "Lorraine Hansberry." *International Dictionary of Theatre 2: Playwrights*. Ed. Mark Hawkins-Dady. Detroit: St. James, 1994. 442-43.

S146   Keppel, Ben. *The Work of Democracy: Ralph Bunche, Kenneth B. Clark, Lorraine Hansberry, and the Cultural Politics of Race*. Cambridge: Harvard UP, 1995.

   Includes two chapters on Hansberry: "The Political Education of Lorraine Hansberry," which examines *A Raisin in the Sun* as a "social document of unappreciated political radicalism and thematic complexity"; and "The Dialectical Imagination of Lorraine Hansberry," which analyzes Hansberry's "efforts to reclaim her text from those who had celebrated it as an affirmation of the American dream." Also includes discussion of *The Drinking Gourd*.

S147   Lee, Dorothy H. "Lorraine Hansberry." *The Gay and Lesbian Literary Heritage*. Ed. Claude J. Summers. New York: Holt, 1995. 356-57.

S148   Miller, Neil. *Out of the Past: Gay and Lesbian History from 1869 to the Present*. New York: Vintage: 1995. 328-32.

S149   Parks, Sheri. "In My Mother's House: Black Feminist Aesthetics, Television, and *A Raisin in the Sun*." *Theatre and Feminist Aesthetics*. Eds. Karen Laughlin, Catherine Schuler. Madison: Fairleigh Dickinson UP, 1995. 200-27.

The 1989 television production of *A Raisin in the Sun*, which reinstated much of what had been cut from the original Broadway production, "placed the play back into the center of black women's concerns for the continuity of the culture and survival of self and family." In a reading of the play from this perspective, suggests that the mass medium of television is useful in conveying the ideas of the "black feminist theatre."

S150   Anon. "Black History Month: Remembering Lorraine Hansberry. *New York Beacon* 7 Feb. 1996: 21.

A biographical review of Hansberry's life with focus on her career as a dramatist. Notes a resurgence of productions of her plays in the 1990's.

S151   Gatewood, Tracy. "Lorraine Hansberry--Still a Name On Stage." *Baltimore Afro-American* 3 March 1996: B10.

A biographical review of Hansberry's life and career.

Dissertations on Hansberry

S152   Friedman, Sharon P. *Feminist Concerns in the Works of Four Twentieth-Century American Women Dramatists: Susan Glaspell, Rachel Crothers, Lillian Hellman, and Lorraine Hansberry*. Dissertation, New York University,

1977. [See *Dissertation Abstracts*, 39 (1977): 858. Order no. AAD78-08567.]

S153 Brown, Elizabeth. *Six Female Black Playwrights: Images of Blacks in Plays by Lorraine Hansberry, Alice Childress, Sonia Sanchez, Barbara Molette, Martie Charles, and Ntozake Shange.* Dissertation, Florida State University, 1980. [See *Dissertation Abstracts* 41 (1980): 3104. Order no. AAD81-00634.]

S154 Grant, Robert Henry. *Lorraine Hansberry: The Playwright as Warrior-Intellectual.* Dissertation, Harvard University, 1982. [See *Dissertation Abstracts* 43 (1982): 1543. Order no. AAD82-22634.]

S155 Turner, S.H. Regina. *Images of Black Women in the Plays of Black Female Playwrights, 1950-1975.* Dissertation, Bowling Green State University, 1982. [See *Dissertation Abstracts* 43 (1982): 19. Order no. AAD82-14438.]

S156 Washington, Rhonnie Lynn. *The Relationship Between the White Critic and the Black Theatre from 1959-1969.* Dissertation, The University of Michigan, 1983. [See *Dissertation Abstracts* 44 (1983): 324. Order no. AAD83-14379.]

S157 Wood, Deborah Jean. *The Plays of Lorraine Hansberry: Studies in Dramatic Form.* Dissertation, The University of Wisconsin-Madison, 1985. [See *Dissertation Abstracts* 46 (1985): 2859. Order no. AAD85-19794.]

S158 Annan, Adaku Tawia. *Revolution as Theater: Revolutionary Aesthetics in the Works of Selected Black Playwrights.* Dissertation, The University of Wisconsin-Madison, 1987. [See *Dissertation Abstracts* 48 (1987): 648. Order no. AAD87-12404.]

S159 Marre, Diana Katherine. *Traditions and Departures: Lorraine Hansberry and Black Americans in Theatre.* Dissertation, University of California-Berkeley, 1987.   [See *Dissertation Abstracts* 48 (1987): 2196.   Order no. AAD87-26290.]

S160   Hardin, Shirley Hodge. *Reconciled and Unreconciled Strivings: A Thematic and Structural Study of the Autobiographies of Four Black Women (Angelou, Brooks, Hansberry, Hurston).* Dissertation, Florida State University, 1988. [See *Dissertation Abstracts* 49 (1988): 1456. Order no. AAD88-14414.]

S161   Humphries, Eugenia. *Lorraine Hansberry: The Visionary American Playwright.* Dissertation, State University of New York at Stony Brook, 1988.   [See *Dissertation Abstracts* 50 (1988): 1305. Order no. AAD89-15503.]

S162   McKelly, James Crisley. *True Wests: Twentieth Century Portraits of the Artist as a Young American.* Dissertation, Indiana University, 1990. [See *Dissertation Abstracts* 52 (1990): 919. Order no. AAD91-22809.]

S163   Stubbs, Mary Frances. *Lorraine Hansberry and Lillian Hellman: A Comparison of Social and Political Issues in Their Plays and Screen Adaptations.*   Dissertation, Indiana University, 1990. [See *Dissertation Abstracts* 51 (1990): 3759. Order no. AAD91-09762.]

S164   Myers, Mary Kay Zettl. *Closure in the Twentieth-Century American Problem Play.* Dissertation, University of Delaware, 1992. [See *Dissertation Abstracts* 53 (1992): 3214. Order no. AAD93-01793.]

S165   Sohn, Hongeal. *Literature and Society: African-American Drama and American Race Relations.* Dissertation, University of Iowa, 1993.

Author Index:
Secondary Bibliographies

The following index lists all critics and scholars included in the secondary bibliographies. The references are keyed to the numbers ("R" = reviews; "S" = books, articles, sections) assigned to the entries.

General Index

The following index records page references as well as references keyed to the primary ("A" = fiction and poetry; "B" = non-fiction; "P" = plays) and secondary ("R" = reviews; "S" = books, articles, and sections) bibliographies.

About the Author

RICHARD M. LEESON is Professor of English at Fort Hays State University in Hays, Kansas. He is the author of *William Inge: A Research and Production Sourcebook* (Greenwood, 1994) as well as numerous articles on American drama and literature.

ISBN 0-313-29312-0

90000>

EAN

9 780313 293122

HARDCOVER BAR CODE